D0904020

A GUIDE TO YOUR HISTORY COURSE

What Every Student Needs To Know

Vincent Alan Clark

Johnson County Community College

Upper Saddle River, New Jersey 07458

Cataloging-in-Publication data available from the Library of Congress.

Executive Editor: Charles Cavaliere
Editorial Assistant: Maureen Diana
Marketing Manager: Laura Lee Manley
Senior Managing Editor (Production):
Mary Carnis
Production Liaison: Marianne Peters-Riordan
Senior Operations Specialist: Mary Ann Gloriande
Cover Art Director: Jayne Conte
Cover Design: Margaret Kenselaar
Cover Photo: Courtesy of
Library of Congress.
Late 19th-century photo of
students in front of the Library of
Congress, Washington, D. C.

Director, Image Resource Center:
Melinda Patelli
Manager, Rights and Permissions:
Zina Arabia
Manager, Visual Research: Beth Brenzel
Manager, Cover Visual Research &
Permissions: Karen Sanatar
Image Permission Coordinator: Annette
Linder
Composition/Full-Service Project
Management: Laserwords/Pine Tree
Composition
Printer/Binder: R.R. Donnelley & Sons
Cover Printer: Coral Graphics

Credits and acknowledgments borrowed from other sources and reproduced, with permission,
in this textbook appear on appropriate page within text.

To the memory of my mother, Elizabeth Marie Bowers Clark,
and to my father, Harold Fenton Clark.

Pearson Education LTD.
Pearson Education Singapore, Pte. Ltd
Pearson Education, Canada, Ltd
Pearson Education–Japan
Pearson Education Australia PTY, Limited

Pearson Education North Asia Ltd
Pearson Educación de Mexico, S.A. de C.V.
Pearson Education Malaysia, Pte. Ltd
Pearson Education, Upper Saddle River,
New Jersey

10 9 8 7 6 5 4 3 2 1
ISBN-10: 0-13-185087-3
ISBN-13: 978-0-13-185087-3

Contents

Preface   *v*

Acknowledgments   *vii*

About the Author   *viii*

Chapter 1   How and When to Use This Book   **1**

Chapter 2   What Is History and Why Is It Important?   **3**
    Why Study History?   3
    What Is History?   6

Chapter 3   Behind the Scenes: The Historians' World   **9**
    Historians' Purposes: Why Historians Study History   10
    What Historians Do   11
    Research and Writing   12
    Evidence   13
    Reliability of Evidence   14
    Interpretations and Debates   15
    Recent Approaches in History   17

Chapter 4   How to Study History   **21**
    General Principles of Effective Study   23
    Textbooks   26
    Lectures   31
    Maps   34
    Primary-Source Documents   36
    Interpretive Essays and Books   38
    Historical Novels and Other Fiction   40
    Paintings, Photographs, and Other Graphic Material   40
    Films and Videotapes   46

Chapter 5   How to Participate Effectively in Class   **50**
    Discussions   51
    Presentations   52
    Group Projects   54

Chapter 6   Success with Tests   **56**
    Studying for Tests   56
    During the Test   59
Chapter 7   Using the Internet to Study History   **64**
    Know How Your History Course Uses the Internet   65
    Use E-Mail Effectively   65
    The World Wide Web   67
    Finding Material on the Internet   69
Chapter 8   How to Write Short Papers for History Classes   **78**
    How to Write Efficiently   79
    Writing Short Essays   83
    Writing Comparisons   84
    Writing Book Reviews   92
Chapter 9   How to Write Research Papers   **97**
    Choosing a Subject   97
    Creating a Bibliography   99
    Planning and Keeping Track of Your Research   100
    Finding Sources   102
    Getting Information and Taking Notes   106
    Organizing Your Paper and Preparing to Write   109
    Writing a First Draft   115
    Revisions, the Final Draft, and Proofreading   115
Chapter 10   How to Cite Your Sources   **117**
    Citations: When, Why, and How to Use Them   117
    Endnote and Footnotes Forms   119
Chapter 11   A Reference Guide to Successful Writing   **136**
    Include a Title   137
    Make the First Sentence Independent of the Title   137
    Every Paper Should Have an Introduction, a Body,
        and a Conclusion   137
    State a Thesis   137
    Use Quotations Effectively   138
    Write Simply   139
    Avoid Jargon and Clichés   140
    Write with a Degree of Formality   140
    Use the Active, Not the Passive, Voice   140
    Use the Past Tense   140
    Write Concisely   141
    Avoid Common Pitfalls   142
    Revise and Proofread   152
Chapter 12   Plagiarism and How to Avoid It   **154**

Credits   **157**
Index   **159**

Preface

University and college students are often like travelers in a foreign country. They can benefit from a guidebook that provides orientation, information about important sites, and helpful information for solving practical problems. This is a student's guidebook to the history course. No matter how seemingly routine to a historian, each course requires intellectual skills, which students must, at some point, learn. Some know them already; many others do not. In the process of taking courses, many students pick up these skills on their own. But many struggle, much to their frustration and that of their instructors, and others would move much more efficiently to the heart of historical study if they had a guide.

As a glance at the contents page will show, this book covers each major type of assignment in college and university history classes, as well as providing material on the value of history, the nature of historical scholarship, and the profession of history. Because of the importance of clear, logical written expression, the book describes in detail the elements of successful writing. Chapters include discussions of short papers and reviews, instructions for writing research papers, and a handy reference guide to important writing principles and common writing problems. Based on students' needs, it also provides three chapters with detailed help on studying all types of material, participating in class, and taking tests. It devotes specific attention to studying artworks, photographs, films, and videotapes. It also contains an extensive and up-to-date section on the use of the Internet in history courses. Finally, two chapters discuss the nature and value of history and describe historical methods, historiography, and the historian's profession.

This guide is designed for the twenty-first-century student who feels pulled in many directions by demands for time. It describes each task in a short section, which students can study when they need to. Students can also read entire chapters or the whole book. Instructors can, therefore, make at least three kinds of assignments. First, an instructor can assign a section as background to a particular assignment. Before students begin a research paper, for example, the instructor could assign the section discussing that task. Second, if the instructor perceives a weakness among specific students or the whole class, she or he might assign a section as a means of remediation. If, for example, some students (or all) seemed to have difficulty writing short essays, the instructor could assign that section. Finally, the instructor could assign the entire book as an introduction to the art and practice of history. This guidebook, then, provides a wide variety of information about the study of history in a highly flexible form.

—Vincent Alan Clark

Acknowledgments

I wish to thank the following reviewers:

Donald R. Abbott, San Diego Mesa College; Kathryn Abbott, Western Kentucky University; Michael J. Galgano, James Madison University; Martin Halpern, Pennsylvania State University, Altoona; Kenneth J. Orosz, University of Maine, Farmington; Steven A. Reich, James Madison University; and Laurie Sprankle, Pennsylvania State University, Altoona.

Any errors or omissions are entirely my own.

About the Author

Vincent Clark received his Ph.D. from the University of California, Riverside. Currently professor of history at Johnson County Community College in suburban Kansas City, he has also taught at the University of San Diego and the University of Kansas. He has been the recipient of two Fulbright Graduate Fellowships to Germany, where he studied at the Institute for Social and Economic History of the University of Heidelberg. His publications include *Living American History*, a book of readings; contributions to *The German Professions, 1800-1950* and *The Educated Middle Class: Educational Systems and Professionalization in International Perspective (Bildungsbürgertum: Bildungssystem und Professionalisierung in internationalen Vergleichen)*; and numerous books reviews. He teaches courses in American, European, and world history and Western civilization.

CHAPTER 1

HOW AND WHEN TO USE THIS BOOK

Anyone who has taken a trip to a foreign country has probably discovered that a good guidebook can be invaluable in telling you where to stay, where to eat, and what to see, especially if you have never been to the country before. Without previous knowledge, new visitors, unfamiliar with a country, discover these things purely by happenstance. They may find good hotels, discover great restaurants, and happen upon interesting sights, but these discoveries are accidental. On the same trip they may also stay in overpriced flea-bag hotels, eat in bad restaurants, and waste time and energy without seeing the most interesting sights. Students in unfamiliar courses may have similar experiences. They may figure out by accident how to succeed, but they may also stumble around not knowing what to do.

This book is designed to be a guidebook to your history class. Based on students' and instructors' experiences, it will guide you through the twists and turns of the college history course. In colleges and universities, history courses require students to do a variety of intellectual tasks. Some students may already know how to do them, others may have only vague notions of what to do, and some may be completely lost. The goal of this book is to show you how to do the major tasks most often required in college history courses.

This book is not designed as another book to read. Instead, it is meant to function as a guidebook. Like a travel guide to France or Italy, you can read it all the way through, or you can also go directly to the information you need. If you have a short paper to write, for example, you can go directly to the appropriate section and read a concise description of how to do that assignment. To help you find the information, this book contains both a detailed table of contents and a list of topics; both are in the beginning of the book. If, for instance, you are assigned to write a research paper, you can go to the table of contents, where you will find a chapter titled "How to Write Research Papers." You can read the whole chapter and get a complete description of the process from beginning to end. It is, of course, a good idea to have such an overall picture, but maybe you just want help in choosing a topic. In the list of subjects you will see a section called "How to Choose a Topic." You can simply go to that and read a couple of pages with specific directions on efficient ways to come up with a subject. You will also find short sections on how to find sources, how to take notes, and how to write your first draft, as well as how to do every other step in the process.

Studying history, like doing anything else, involves certain skills. This book is designed to describe them to you, quickly and efficiently. The goal is to help you be successful, so that you can enjoy the study of history.

CHAPTER 2

WHAT IS HISTORY AND WHY IS IT IMPORTANT?

AT A GLANCE

Why Study History?
- Interest in the past is a human characteristic.
- Studying history helps us understand ourselves.
- History is essential for understanding our world.
- History is an important tool for understanding other people.
- History can help you in everyday life.
- History can be recreation.

What Is History?
- History is the study of the past, which can encompass all periods, from the ancient to the very recent.
- History includes all subjects, from politics to popular music.
- Historians look for the significance of their findings.

WHY STUDY HISTORY?

This book is designed to help you get the most out of your history class. But why study history at all? And why do colleges—and even business schools—require students to take it?

Let us begin with the curious fact that almost all human beings have some kind of interest in the past. A sense of history, in fact, may be a characteristic of being human. To use a commonplace example, when people get together, they spend a great deal of time telling stories; most conversations, in fact, are full of them. Stories, of course, are about the past, and in a sense, therefore, almost everyone is a historian of sorts.

People's interest in history, of course, goes far beyond mere storytelling. In most tribal societies, people recite lists of ancestors. Almost as soon as the ancient Chinese developed writing, they began to write history. And in every advanced society since then, people have been recording, writing, and reading history.

Why did they do this, and why do we? A philosophical answer might be that knowing our history informs our sense of ourselves, and in retelling it, we give ourselves an identity, a significance, an importance. A more obvious, if prosaic, reason is that it gives us pleasure, as the perpetual storytelling in our conversations shows. Knowing the past can also help us understand ourselves. Perhaps, for example, your parents went through a divorce, which affected you deeply. Exploring that part of your history might help you understand the kind of person you are today. Perhaps you suffered traumas in high school, and you still feel inadequate and unpopular today. Without getting too deeply into armchair psychology, it seems safe to say that examining that part of your history might be useful. Perhaps, on the other hand, your dominant experiences were more positive: Your parents made you feel successful; you were popular in high school; you got good grades; a teacher told you that you had writing talent. These experiences—these aspects of your *history*—have influenced you and helped make you the kind of person you are. Whatever the case, it is useful to understand them, to know your own personal history.

Seeing the relationship of your personal history to that of the larger society might be valuable as well. For one thing, your experience might be part of a larger trend. You might, for example, discover that your parents' divorce was part of a late-twentieth-century divorce epidemic, and, as a result, understand your parents better—and yourself. Or maybe a family member was killed in the Vietnam War and your family is still affected by that death. Knowing something about the war and its effects on American society might make it easier to understand what happened to your family. In short, understanding how your history fits into that of your society and country can further help you understand yourself.

At our best, however, and as educated people, we want to know more than just ourselves. We need to understand how our society functions; as citizens we need to know how our political system works. We cannot, for example, understand why we elect presidents as we do without understanding the origins of the electoral college. Nor is it possible to understand current race relations without knowing something about slavery and the history of legal discrimination. In fact, almost every current debate requires historical knowledge. Is crime getting worse? Is the American family falling apart? Are politicians getting more dishonest? The only way to answer these questions is to know how things were before, to study the past—in short, to study history.

We also want to know about other people, including those different from ourselves. To do that, we have to know their history. If, for example, we want to understand Russia, we must know something about its history, including the fact that except for a very short time, before the fall of communism in the early 1990s, it has had no experience with popularly elected government. Or how can we make sense of what is happening in the Middle East? We have to look at its history, how it got to be the way it is, what experiences its people have gone through. In short, knowing history is essential for knowing both ourselves and the world around us.

Many people, of course, accept the value of historical knowledge, often citing philosopher George Santayana's hoary (and frequently misquoted) apothegm that "Those who cannot remember the past are condemned to repeat it."[1] Conceivably, historical knowledge could prevent the repetition of past mistakes, or at least induce a healthy sense of caution. In the late 1990s, for example, stock market enthusiasts trumpeted the emergence of a supposed "New Economy," created by the Internet and immune, they claimed, to the ups and downs of the business cycle. The stock market, they predicted, would go up forever. Some of the most optimistic even predicted a Dow-Jones average of 30,000—three times its actual high. When the market fell in 2000–2001, a lot of people lost big.

Proponents of the Santayana view would suggest that these investors might well have remembered the 1920s. At that time stock market experts called the period "the New Era" and claimed that new growth industries (automobiles and home appliances) had eliminated the business cycle—and the possibility of a stock market crash. The lesson seems obvious. But as the dot.com market bubble shows, many people found it hard to remember.

Often, however, using history to avoid mistakes is not as easy as it seems. Everyone wants to avoid repeating Napoleon's attack on Russia, the Western allies' failure to stop Hitler in the 1930s, and the Vietnam War. But few situations correspond exactly to past events. What lesson, for example, should we draw from the allies' inaction in the face of Hitler's expansion? That nations should always use force against aggressive dictators? But when the world is full of such dictators, which ones should we resist? Many historians, moreover, have argued that it was precisely American desires to apply this lesson—to resist what seemed like the expansionism of communist dictatorship—that led to the Vietnam War. And, by the way, what are the lessons of Vietnam?

In seeking to learn from the past, we might be on firmer ground if we used history to look at long-term trends, aware, of course, that even here we should exercise caution. In the modern world such trends include wholesale population movements from rural to urban areas and a shriveling number of farmers: In most industrialized countries, including the United States, they now amount to 5 percent or less of the population. Seeing such trends can help us understand the present. They can also guide policy decisions, such as what to do about farm subsidies. And, obviously, they can be instructive for voters.

Now a couple of other reasons to study history: On a utilitarian level, it can provide you with invaluable skills for everyday life. History classes teach a host of them: how to find facts, how to evaluate sources, how to differentiate good from bad information, how to present your findings and ideas in coherent and persuasive ways. Knowing how to find information and evaluate it can help you decide which car or washing machine to buy. Knowing how to find and evaluate facts and present your findings can help you in your career in business, government, or a nonprofit agency.

Finally, history can enrich your life, even on the level of fun. Millions of people read history in their spare time for recreation. History books often appear on best-seller lists. People travel hundreds, even thousands, of miles to historic battlegrounds and other sites. And towns, cities, and states, knowing how history attracts tourists (and their money), proudly label their historic sites and museums and spend millions of dollars each year promoting them.

WHAT IS HISTORY?

We have already seen that history, to put it briefly, is the study of the past. The word *past* may conjure up Romans in togas and medieval knights jousting on a battlefield. Actually, though, the past—the stuff of history—consists of everything right up to and including the most recent previous moment. It therefore encompasses almost everything we know.

Some historians, in fact, specialize in the recent past. German historians have even coined a term for this specialization: *Zeitgeschichte*, or the history of our time. Studying the very recent past, however, presents potential problems. One is the difficulty of establishing adequate perspective. Another is evidence. To a large extent, historians rely on documents, written evidence, which often shows the motivation of historical figures. For a number of reasons—ranging from the preservation of personal privacy to the safeguarding of national security—most nations, including the United States, restrict access to recent sensitive documents. In addition, powerful figures, like American presidents, who control documents often resist releasing them.

History includes not only the whole spectrum of time, from ancient to recent; it also encompasses every human activity. Historians study not only politics, diplomacy, and war, but also popular music, movies, sports, photography, psychology, science, drinking, and sex. If you are interested in any area of human activity, you are interested in history, whether you know it or not.

In examining these areas, professional historians use the historical method—or, more accurately, historical methods. These involve finding evidence, examining its reliability and value, establishing facts, and determining their meaning, or significance. Historians also, of course, present their findings, usually in writing.

Most historians are more interested in the significance of their findings than simply in facts themselves. An examination of historical writing shows that significance can take several forms. Among them is the reconceptualization of historic developments. The work of the American historian Patricia Limerick provides an example. One of the so-called New Western Historians, Limerick has attempted a radical revision of the common picture of the "winning" of the American West. Like others in her informal group, she rejects the stereotypical view of the West as an empty land of wide-open spaces tamed by heroic white cowboys and other pioneers. In her portrayal it was not empty but inhabited. The inhabitants, of course, included Indians as well as Hispanic settlers and their descendants, who had lived in the Southwest for generations. Her view, therefore, stresses the West's ethnic diversity. Further, it portrays the white English-speaking settlement of the West as a conquest, a subjugation—in many cases, a near extermination—of peoples living in the region. Finally, Limerick's work also emphasizes the destruction of the natural environment, as well as the class divisions and class conflict that accompanied the settlement.[2]

Gary Nash and, later, Edward Countryman have pursued similar themes in examining the colonial period. In his book *Red, White, and Black*, for example, Nash has attempted to dispel the notion that early American history was primarily the story of European settlers. For him it is rather the interaction—often unwilling—of native, African, and European Americans.[3] Countryman, too, has sought to assert the multinational and multicultural character of this period.[4]

Another type of significance is the fit between a historical development and a historical theory. In the 1950s and 1960s, the English historian Christopher Hill attempted to show that the English Civil War of the 1640s, when Parliament overthrew and later executed King Charles I, was an expression of class warfare in the Marxist sense.[5] As might be expected, many historians disagreed with Hill, arguing, in the process, for their own concept of significance.

Another form of significance that historians sometimes develop is attributing responsibility for catastrophic events. In the early 1960s the German historian Fritz Fischer published a book attempting to show that contrary to the views of most previous German historians, the German government bore a large share of the blame for the outbreak of World War I.[6] A similar attribution of blame appeared recently in the work of John Lewis Gaddis. In reevaluating the Cold War between the Western and Soviet blocs after World War II, Gaddis recently asserted that responsibility rests with "authoritarianism in general and Stalin in particular."[7]

Closely related to such attributions of responsibility is the assessment of historical figures. For example, Joseph Ellis, in his book *American Sphinx*, condemns Thomas Jefferson for failing to embrace an activist concept of the federal government.[8] As you can see, in most cases the significance is far more important than mere facts—and usually more interesting as well. If you are interested in more information about how professional historians work, please read Chapter 3, "Behind the Scenes: How Professional Historians Work."

QUICK REVIEW

- **Why study history?** An interest in the past is an aspect of being human. History helps us understand ourselves, other people, and the world. History can also help us in everyday life, and can be an ongoing source of pleasure.

- **What is history?** History is the study of the past, which encompasses all periods from the ancient to the very recent. It includes all subjects, from politics to popular music. And it is more than merely amassing facts—it involves a search for significance of developments in the past.

NOTES

1. George Santayana, *The Life of Reason* (Project Guttenberg, 2005), vol. 1, chap. 12, http://www.gutenberg.org/files/15000/15000-h/vol1.html.

2. Patricia Limerick, *The Legacy of Conquest: The Unbroken Past of the American West* (New York: Norton, 1987).

3. Gary B. Nash, *Red, White, and Black: The Peoples of Early America*, 2nd ed. (Englewood Cliffs, N.J.: Prentice Hall, 1982).

4. Edward Countryman, *Americans: A Collision of Histories* (New York: Hill and Wang, 1996).

5. See, for example, Christopher Hill, *The World Turned Upside Down: Radical Ideas during the English Revolution* (London: Temple Smith, 1972).

6. Fritz Fischer, *Germany's Aims in the First World War*, trans. James Joll (London: Chatto & Windus, 1967).

7. John Lewis Gaddis, *We Know Now: Rethinking Cold War History* (New York: Oxford University Press, 1997), 294.

8. Joseph J. Ellis, *American Sphinx: The Character of Thomas Jefferson* (New York: Alfred A. Knopf, 1997).

CHAPTER 3

BEHIND THE SCENES: THE HISTORIAN'S WORLD

AT A GLANCE

Why historians study history
- Historians devote their professional lives to history because of their fascination with it. In addition, most believe that understanding history is essential for understanding the present.

What historians do
- Most historians work in academic institutions: colleges and universities.
- At major research universities they devote major efforts to research and writing; at liberal arts and community colleges, they spend most of their time in teaching and related work.
- Other historians work in nonacademic institutions, such as museums, archives, the armed forces, and corporations. Some are independent scholars and writers.

Research and writing
- Scholarly writing can take the form of monographs, works of synthesis, and book reviews.

Evidence
- Since evidence is the foundation of history, its nature and quality are very important to all historians.

(continued)

> **Interpretation and Debate**
> - At its heart, history is a series of dialogues—debates—about evidence, conclusions, and the proper objects of historical study.
>
> **Recent trends in history**
> - Since the 1960s, historians have been particularly interested in social history—the study of ordinary people.
> - Prominent recent interests include gender, environmental, and global history.

Many students see their history professors primarily in the public role of conducting classes. But you may have some inkling that there is more than that to the job. You may wonder what your professor and other historians really do. Maybe you have heard about historians' rating of American presidents or read about historical discoveries, like the papers from Abraham Lincoln's legal practice, which are now being collected. Perhaps you have even thought about becoming a historian yourself. What is involved? What is the historian's job like? This chapter will take you behind the scenes and give you a glimpse into the world of historians and the modern historical profession.

HISTORIANS' PURPOSES: WHY HISTORIANS STUDY HISTORY

Most historians, it is safe to say, devote their professional lives to history because they are fascinated with it. Most also believe that knowing the past is essential for understanding the present. Historians who study slavery in the United States, for example, usually believe that knowing about this institution helps us understand race relations in twenty-first-century America. Likewise, those who study family history believe that this knowledge helps us understand what is going on in the modern American family. Even those who study societies that have disappeared, "worlds we have lost,"[1] in the words of the late English historian Peter Laslett, believe that these societies tell us something important about the present. For example, knowing that work in the preindustrial world was not continuous and machine-like—as it is in factories and offices today—but came in spurts of long, intense work at times like harvesting followed by periods of relative idleness, helps us understand the stresses of modern society. At the very least, many of these historians would argue, this knowledge shows us that our current working lives are not a given, are not the only possible way to work, and that if people in the past worked differently, we might be able to restructure our work as well. In addition to its ability to illuminate the present, history also fascinates most historians for its own sake.

Whether they study traditional China, medieval Europe, or the American Civil War, most find the actions of human beings in the past engrossing.

WHAT HISTORIANS DO

As you may have surmised, most historians work in academic institutions: colleges and universities. Most spend a great deal of their time teaching; the amount varies with the type of college or university. In major research institutions, like the University of California, Yale, and the University of Chicago, historians have relatively small teaching loads—often one or two classes per semester—to give them time for research and writing. At universities with less emphasis on research, and at many liberal arts and community colleges, faculty members usually devote more time to teaching and less to research. Teaching, of course, entails much more than leading classes; it also involves preparing class sessions and tests, grading, talking with students, and writing letters of recommendation. In addition to teaching, most professors also serve on committees involved in decision making in their departments and institutions. Like academics in other disciplines, some historians serve as college and university administrators. Recently, for example, Drew Gilpin Faust, a prominent historian specializing in the Civil War and the American South, recently became president of Harvard University.

Other historians have nonteaching positions. Some work in museums, libraries, and archives. Others work for government agencies, like the Army, Navy, and Air Force, or large private companies. A few historians devote all or almost all of their time to research and writing. One of these is Garry Wills, a prolific author of numerous highly regarded books, such as *Lincoln at Gettysburg*, which won the Pulitzer Prize for history in 1993.

Almost all historians are specialists in certain fields of history. Among those working in the United States, the largest field, not surprisingly, is American history. In 2001–2002, according to a survey by the American Historical Association, 39 percent of all historians specialized in this area. The second largest field is European history. The same survey showed that those specializing in this field amounted to 26 percent of the total. These two areas were by far the largest specialties among historians in the United States. No other field—East Asia, Africa, the Middle East—comprised even 10 percent of the total.[2]

Regardless of the region they study, historians usually divide history into chronological periods. They break European history, for example, into medieval, early modern (ca. 1450–1789), and modern (ca. 1789 to the present) and make further subdivisions within each of them. Individual historians usually focus their research on even smaller periods; in U.S. history, for example, on the Civil War, Reconstruction (the period immediately following the Civil War), or some other relatively short period. Most historians also specialize in some specific type of history, like military, diplomatic, political, labor, gender, or environmental; this list, however, is not exhaustive, and other possibilities exist.

Most historians also have at least one additional area of expertise outside their main field of specialization. These outside areas usually go back to the historian's graduate education, where they were required. For example, a historian's primary area of specialization might be modern Europe with secondary fields in early modern European and twentieth-century U.S. history. Many graduate schools also require historians to study fields outside history. A budding historian might, for example, choose religion, economics, or sociology (all are related to history).

RESEARCH AND WRITING

In addition to teaching, many historians also conduct research and write scholarly books and articles. Such writing can take several different forms. The basic type is the monograph: an article or book on a single subject based on original research. Since monographs employ original research in primary sources, they form the foundation of historical writing. A distinguished example is the biography of the African-American historian, sociologist, and political thinker W. E. B. Du Bois by David Levering Lewis, which has won numerous awards, including the Pulitzer Prize for history in 1994.

At the opposite end of the spectrum are works of synthesis, which rely on already-published material but advance new interpretations of a period, or even of the whole history of a country. An example is *Americans,* a 1996 book by Edward Countryman of Southern Methodist University, in which the author wove together the historical elements that he thought made Americans as a people distinctive. Another example is *China: A New History* by the late John King Fairbank of Harvard, who argued that a basic defect of Chinese history was the failure to develop any tradition of rights or representative government (a view many would see as excessively Eurocentric).

Works of historical scholarship vary considerably in scope. Some deal with a single person or even a single incident, like the Salem witchcraft trials. Others attempt to cover wide swaths of a country's history, like David Hackett Fischer's *Albion's Seed: Four British Folkways in America,* which argued that all American history is derived from four British regional subcultures, which became established in New England, Pennsylvania, the coastal South, and the Southern highlands.

Historians often write reviews of books in their areas of specialization. These usually run from 400 to 800 words and appear in professional historical journals—those read primarily by other historians—like the *American Historical Review,* the *Journal of American History,* and the *Journal of Modern History.* These reviews typically summarize new books, compare them with similar books on the same subject, and evaluate them. For historians trying to stay up to date in their fields, reviews are invaluable. In modern German history, for example, several hundred scholarly works appear each year, and most historians have nowhere near the time necessary to read all of them, especially while at the same time teaching and perhaps doing their own research. Professional journals, most of which come out four times a year, therefore, usually contain a substantial number of reviews in each issue. A recent issue of the *American Historical Review*, for example, contained 186 book reviews. With four issues per year, therefore, this journal would publish close to eight hundred book reviews annually. Because of their extensive reading and writing, most historians place high value on the written word and are often connoisseurs of good writing. Besides esteem for precise and graceful expression, many historians see themselves as heirs of their society's storytelling traditions. And, as many students have discovered, they are often exacting critics of student writing and view the red pen as an important professional tool.

EVIDENCE

The foundation of history is evidence. Without it historians might as well be writing fiction. Since it is so important, a historian must cite sources (in a foot- or endnotes) so that readers (often other historians) can identify and judge these sources and the way the author uses them. Sources are so important that when historians write, they often discuss them in detail. In some cases, readers double checking evidence have found serious errors. In just the past few years they have caught authors reversing the original meaning of sources or being unable to show where their information came from. These cases have serious consequences for errant historians, often leading to forced resignation or dismissal from academic positions.

The most valuable evidence usually consists of original documents, which historians call primary sources. These are materials produced at the time in history under consideration. They may be the official texts of legislation, government officials' memoranda, letters, articles in newspapers and magazines, or diaries of important or common people. In recent years, for example, social historians have sought the diaries and other papers of ordinary people, sometimes discovering items of great value for understanding how they lived and thought. In the early 1980s, for example, the historian Laurel Thatcher Ulrich came upon the two-volume diary of Martha Ballard, a midwife who lived in Augusta, Maine, and wrote during the years 1785 to 1812. In Ulrich's hands the diary turned into a source of insight into ordinary life in northern New England, women's roles, and health and medicine. After eight years of work Ulrich published a book, *A Midwife's Tale*, which won the Pulitzer Price for history and the Bancroft Prize, given by Columbia University for the outstanding book in American history.

For the historian one of the tricks is discovering what primary sources exist and where they are. Sometimes this is relatively easy. For example, a historian studying a political event like the introduction and passage of the Social Security Act during the New Deal could find transcripts of the debates in both the House and the Senate in the *Congressional Record* and could read letters and memoranda by President Franklin D. Roosevelt and officials of his administration in the National Archives. In fact, documents for the study of political developments are often relatively easy to find. Many governments publish collections of important diplomatic documents; legislatures publish transcripts of their proceedings; and the U.S. government has published important papers from presidential administrations, which you can find in university libraries. Often, however, documents take more work to find. Some are available in archives (institutions that store historical material), but the researcher must determine which archive they are in and travel there to look at them. Frequently, the contents of the documents are unknown until the researcher sees them firsthand. And sometimes it is hard to find if any relevant documents exist and, if so, where they are.

Recently, the Internet has brought some primary sources as close as researchers' own computers, with archives, libraries, and museums digitizing materials and displaying them on Web sites. Historians of the ancient Mediterranean have benefited particularly from this process. The entire Dead Sea Scrolls, for instance, are now on the Internet, and many inscriptions, which provide valuable information to Greek and Roman historians, are also available.

RELIABILITY OF EVIDENCE

Historians must always be alert to problems with documents. The first danger is the fallibility of the document's author. Even eyewitnesses can be mistaken, and anyone can err because of bias, emotional involvement, or other reasons. In addition, of course, most people want to put their actions in the best possible light and may, consciously or unconsciously, shade what they say accordingly. Government officials may be especially prone to such distortions. An observer or interpreter's worldview may also shape perceptions. Historians must, therefore, exercise care in interpreting evidence and drawing conclusions. They must, to use an old saying, consider the source.

This means testing evidence for consistency and attempting to corroborate it with other sources. Those working in some specialized fields have developed tests based on the nature of the material. But in judging evidence, historians sometimes make mistakes. In 1983 the late English historian Hugh Trevor-Roper (who had become Lord Dacre) declared a group of documents purporting to be Adolf Hitler's diaries to be authentic. Subsequent examination by other experts showed them to be frauds, much to Trevor-Roper's embarrassment. (The ink and paper used, for example, were manufactured after Hitler's death.)

Historians' work, therefore, usually undergoes several stages of expert scrutiny and revision. Historians often first present their work as papers at scholarly conferences for other historians' comments. After that, a paper may undergo revision—sometimes many revisions—before submission to a scholarly publication, like the *Journal of Modern History* (for European historians) or the *Journal of American History* (for specialists in U.S. history). Before publishing it, however, the editors will send it to experts in the field for review.

Hitler diary forger Konrad Kujau, with the "diaries" and his lawyer (right).

To preserve their freedom to comment objectively, these reviewers are usually anonymous. They are expected to raise any questions or objections they may have to the work. If these are serious, the editor may ask the author to make revisions. If the revisions are satisfactory, the article can then be published. Even after publication, however, other scholars may criticize its methods or conclusions.

Eventually, the work may appear in a book. Before publication, however, experts will again review it, and the editor may ask for revisions. Books sometimes will fail to pass reviewers' muster and are rejected for publication. When a book is published, however, its exposure to criticism continues. Professional journals review most books, and in the reviews, scholars point out the flaws they perceive. Reviews of historical books may also appear in nonspecialist publications, like the *New Republic*, or even prominent newspapers like the *New York Times*—where critics will examine them again.

INTERPRETATIONS AND DEBATES

For professional historians, history is not so much amassing facts as, like other scholarly disciplines, participating in a series of debates. Historians, for example, debate the nature of the Cold War between the Western and Soviet blocs, the character of American slavery, the cause of World War I, and the reasons Hitler came to power. The goal of such debates is consensus, which for a variety of reasons is not always reached. The study of historical scholarship and debate is called historiography. Historians are not alone in refining their knowledge in this way. Sociologists, anthropologists, and even natural scientists, like biologists and physicists, do the same thing. The ferment of historical debate leads to new approaches to historical study, new interpretations, new subjects, and new kinds of history. Young historians in particular eagerly seek new areas of research and writing. Not only are they exciting, they can make a historian's career.

Historians' debates are not just about the facts, which may or may not be in dispute. They are primarily about interpretation—the way in which historians understand and present the facts. Interpretations change over time. A classic example is the interpretation of Reconstruction, the period after the American Civil War in which the former Confederate states were reintegrated into the Union. During the late nineteenth and early twentieth centuries most historians described the new Southern state government, which brought blacks into politics, as viciously corrupt. To these historians, the Northerners who had moved south were opportunistic Carpetbaggers, the Southern whites allied with them were traitorous Scalawags, and the blacks were ignorant and animalistic. The white politicians who eventually seized power from this group and imposed racial segregation were "Redeemers," who saved the "good white people" of the South from these exploiters. With the rise of the civil rights movement in the 1950s, however, historians began to abandon that interpretation. Viewing racial segregation as a great national evil, they reexamined Reconstruction governments and saw them in a much more positive light. They viewed the "Redeemers," who had imposed racial segregation on the South, as the villains of the piece. Such shifts have taken place in the interpretation of other developments and in the histories of many countries.

Historical debates have many causes. Records are often incomplete or insufficient. Disagreements result from political and ideological differences. Marxists, for example, believe that economic interests drive events, while historians of other persuasions believe that culture or ideas are more important. Other perspectives, often based on historians' background and experiences, can affect their view.

The political situation can also affect the way historians view the past. Before World War II the inequities of industrial societies led the so-called Progressive historians to view American history as essentially a series of conflicts between the rich and the ordinary people. However, the Cold War—the atomic standoff between the Western and the Soviet blocs following World War II—caused many in the next generation to see American society in a more sanguine light. In the face of the apparent threat of totalitarian dictatorship, many began to view the United States as a society that despite its defects had been remarkably successful in creating unprecedented levels of democracy and prosperity.

In the late 1960s, however, the pendulum swung back again. The civil rights and antiwar movements led many to a more pessimistic view of American history.

Racial discrimination, which many now fought, pointed to the history of racial injustice; and what seemed to many an unjust war called new attention to historic flaws in American foreign policy. A new group of historians much more critical of the American past emerged.

RECENT APPROACHES IN HISTORY

Human beings have always been interested in their past, and most literate societies have had historians. In the Western world the writing of history can be traced back to the Greek historians Herodotus and Thucydides; Chinese historical writing is thought to have begun with Sima Tan and his son Sima Qian; and most other advanced societies have also had important historians. In the United States and many other countries, the late nineteenth century saw the emergence of professional historians—men and women who received specialized training in history and pursued it as their principal occupation. Previously, most of those writing history had been amateurs, having received no specific training in history and deriving their incomes from some other source, such as the church or the practice of law. The new professional historians earned Ph.D.s and were especially influenced by the development of modern historical study in Germany under such scholars as Leopold von Ranke, who stressed critical analysis of sources and objective description of the past.

Many historians of this period, like J. B. Bury of Britain, saw history as part of a great scientific enterprise, which encompassed not only the natural sciences like biology and physics, but also the new social sciences of sociology and psychology. As a science, these historians believed, history should use the scientific method, developed in the natural sciences. This would involve the careful, dispassionate examination of the evidence and the submission of conclusions in the form of scholarly papers, articles, and books, for evaluation by colleagues. If the work survived this review, it would form part of an edifice of historical knowledge, upon which subsequent historians would build.

Many subsequent historians, however, have rejected the notion of history as an impartial, objective compilation of facts. For Marxists, economics and class influence all thought, including the writing of history, making the notion of historical objectivity naïve. Other philosophical ideas have also cast doubt on the possibility of impartiality.

In recent years, history, like many other disciplines, has felt the influence of postmodernism, which views objectivity as illusory. Instead, postmodernists see all forms of language, including the documents that historians rely on and the writing of history itself, as politically motivated. For them the task of historians is to analyze the political forces behind the documents and to lay them bare in their writing.

Traditionally, history has concerned itself with high politics: with the affairs of governments and rulers, with kings, presidents, prime ministers, diplomats, with war and the making of peace. In the late nineteenth and early twentieth centuries these matters continued to occupy the attention of most professional historians. Ranke, for example, insisted on the "primacy of politics."[3]

By the 1960s, however, many historians began moving in a new direction, espousing what they called social history. This focused not on the social elites, who usually dominated politics, but on common people, especially the poor, who had often seemed invisible in previous historical writing. Certain social groups—peasants, factory workers, and slaves—attracted extensive attention from such historians, partly because they comprised large proportions of the ordinary population. These groups have also loomed large in certain historical theories, especially that of Marxism. Other occupational groups have also attracted attention, partly because they, too, have been seen as victims of oppression. Recently, for example, even prostitutes have attracted historians' attention (e.g., *City of Eros: New York City, Prostitution, and the Commercialization of Sex* by Timothy J. Gilfoyle).

While deemphasizing high politics, social historians have often concentrated on political movements among common people. For example, in his 1963 book *The Making of the English Working Class*, the English historian E. P. Thompson sought to show that an industrial working class, corresponding to the Marxist model, emerged in early nineteenth-century England. Social historians have also attempted to portray the working lives of ordinary people. In the book *Women at Work*, for example, the American historian Thomas Dublin portrayed the lives of young women in the textile factories of Lowell, Massachusetts, in the 1820s and 1830s. Another American historian, Paul Johnson, described the effect of a religious movement—the Second Great Awakening—on the people of Rochester, New York, during approximately the same period. He showed that the movement tended to appeal to upwardly mobile workmen more than others and found support among factory owners because it seemed to promise a more disciplined workforce.

Social historians are interested in a wide range of other aspects of ordinary people's lives, many of which are also studied by sociologists. Social mobility—the movement of people upward and downward in society—is one such area. In the mid-1960s Stephen Thernstrom wrote a pioneering study of social mobility in Boston. European historians have also been interested in this subject; David Crew, for example, has made an extensive study of social mobility in a German industrial city in his book *Town in the Ruhr: A Social History of Bochum, 1860–1914*. Another important aspect of everyday life that has attracted the attention of social historians is health. Richard Evans, for instance, has written an illuminating account of the effects of cholera epidemics in Hamburg, Germany, in the years 1830–1910. Health, of course, was an important subject in Laura Thatcher Ulrich's book on Martha Ballard. Social historians have also begun studying sexual behavior, a subject that seems to have unlimited interest for human beings. In the 1970s, for example, Edward Shorter studied sexual behavior among Europeans in his book *The Making of the Modern Family*. Historians have also devoted extensive study to marriage and family life.

United States historians have long studied slavery. For those specializing in more recent periods, race—and, more broadly, ethnicity—is an important subject. Class, too, has long occupied social historians, especially those influenced by Marxism, and for many this continues to be an important subject of investigation. Finally, the issue of gender has attracted a great deal of interest from historians. With the emergence of the women's movement in the 1960s, the history of women developed as an area of historical study for historians of all regions and has resulted in numerous important books.

The study of women's history led historians to examine the changing concept of what being a woman meant in various times and societies. The insights from this study led in turn to a similar approach to the concepts of masculinity, what it meant to be a man, say, in mid-nineteenth-century America. This field has now attracted a good deal of attention and has produced a number of interesting books, among them *Making Manhood: Growing Up Male in Colonial New England* by Anne S. Lombard. Like the women's movement, the gay rights movement also developed in the 1960s and gave rise to the historical study of homosexuals and other persons previously viewed as deviant. Increasingly, historians working in both of these fields have called for the employment of the concept of gender, which they often see as a social construct imposed on people or chosen by them—rather than a biological given.

Another recent specialty is environmental history. In 1979 Professor Donald Worster, now of the University of Kansas, published *Dust Bowl: The Southern Plains in the 1930s*, which chronicled the Dust Bowl and its catastrophic environmental results. Subsequently, other historians have explored other aspects of environmental history. Recent books in this field include *On the Great Plains: Agriculture and Environment*, by Geoff Cunfer; *This Delta, This Land: An Environmental History of the Yazoo–Mississippi Floodplain*, by Mikko Saikku; and *Crow's Range: An Environmental History of the Sierra Nevada*, by David Beesley. Historians have written environmental histories of other regions as well. For example, in 2003, I. G. Simmons published the *Moorlands of England and Wales: An Environmental History 8000 BC to AD 2000*. The next year Christopher A. Conte moved the genre into African history, publishing *Highland Sanctuary: Environmental History in Tanzania's Usambara Mountains*. And the same year saw the publication of Mark Elvin's *Retreat of the Elephants: An Environmental History of China*.

A further trend affecting historical writing today is comparative history, the attempt to compare developments in one area with those in others, to achieve, if possible, a worldwide perspective on historical developments. Some historians have long been interested in making comparisons, but the new interest in comparative history proceeds partly from the increasing consciousness of the interrelatedness of the world and a desire to avoid an exclusive focus on the historian's own culture. This interest appears in most areas of specialization but especially in the history of the United States.

Most students see historians primarily as conducting their history classes. That is certainly an important role, but for many historians it is only the public face of what goes on behind the scenes. As this brief glimpse has shown, historians are ultimately involved in a debate over the nature of the past and its meaning for the present.

QUICK REVIEW

* **Historians study history because** of their fascination with it; most also believe it is essential for understanding the present.
* **Most historians work** in academic institutions: colleges and universities. At major research universities they devote their primary efforts to research and writing; at liberal arts and community colleges, they spend most of their time in teaching and related work. Others work in nonacademic institutions, such as museums, archives, the armed forces, and corporations.
* **Research and writing** can result in monographs, works of synthesis, and book reviews.
* **Since evidence is the foundation of history**, its nature and quality are important to all historians.
* **History is a series of debates**—about evidence, conclusions, and the proper objects of historical study.
* **Recent trends in history** include social history, with much current interest devoted to gender, environmental, and global history.

NOTES

1. Peter Laslett, *The World We Have Lost* (New York: Scribner, 1965).
2. Robert B. Townsend, "The State of the History Department: The 2001–02 AHA Department survey," *Perspectives Online* 42 (April 2004): 4; *http://www .historians.org/perspectives/issues/2004/0404/.*
3. See Wolfgang J. Mommsen, "Domestic Factors in German Foreign Policy before 1914," *Central European History* 6 (1973): 3–4.

CHAPTER 4

HOW TO STUDY HISTORY

AT A GLANCE

General Principles
- Look for the important points.
- Use your memory effectively.
- Manage your time.

Textbooks
- Survey the material before reading it.
- Identify the important points.
- Use effective techniques to learn the material.
- Review.

Lectures
- Note the important points.
- Take effective notes.
- Study your notes efficiently.

Maps
- Understand what the map is showing.
- Know the point (or points) the map is trying to make.

(continued)

Primary-Source Documents
- Follow any special directions from your instructor.
- Know who wrote the document, when it was written, what the main points are, and what it tells you about the period, events, or personalities under discussion.

Interpretive Essays and Books
- Know the author's thesis and supporting arguments.
- To evaluate the work, examine when the material was written, whether the evidence is persuasive, how it compares with other writing on the subject, and how it accords with your own thinking.

Historical Novels and Other Fiction
- Consider how the work portrays the period and events described.
- Compare it to what you have learned from other sources.

Paintings, Photographs, and Other Graphic Material
- Look for information the work reveals about the period, the viewpoint of the work, and the possible manipulation of images.
- Put important facts in your notes.
- Use effective learning principles.

Film and Videotapes
- If nonfiction, take notes and study as you would for lectures.
- If a feature film, study it as you would historical fiction, being alert to the interpretation.

It is no secret that success in a college course requires effective study. No one trying to master a subject has yet found a substitute for study. But how should you study? Before looking at specific techniques, note that studying history means more than simply memorizing facts. Historical knowledge involves understanding societies and human beings of the past and how they changed over time. Studying, moreover, requires more than simply reading a textbook. It requires perceiving concepts, thinking about them critically, and being able to discuss them, especially in writing. Such an approach requires a substantial investment of time—more than many students initially realize. The results, however, are well worth the investment. Not only does this kind of study lead to higher grades; it also provides a sense of mastery, a familiarity with the riches of the past, and an understanding of continuity and change in the human condition.

GENERAL PRINCIPLES OF EFFECTIVE STUDY

Several principles underlie the effective study of all types of college history assignments. This section describes these general concepts, and the remainder of the chapter explains effective techniques for studying specific types of material assigned in history courses.

1. Look for the Important Points, Not Just Facts

Many students see history as a mass of facts, which they think they have to memorize. But when historians write, they are interested less in piling up facts than in advancing ideas. When you study, therefore, you should concentrate on the important points and make them the focus of your studying.

But what are the important points? In general, historical writing contains three levels of points, each of which you should study. The first contains the thesis or a theme. Some kinds of writing—articles, for example, discussed later in this chapter—usually contain a thesis statement, a summary of the author's principal point. Others, like textbooks or textbook chapters, may have a theme, an overarching approach that unifies the material.

On the second level are major points, which, though less central than a thesis or theme, are still important. In articles and books, such points may support a thesis. In textbooks, which are usually devoted more to description than to advancing arguments, they can form the primary content of the work. On a third level are points that support, elaborate, illustrate, or qualify more general points. The following selection from a world history textbook illustrates these second- and third-level points. In this selection, which discusses early Chinese societies, the author, Howard Spodek, has just described the Yanshao people. He now moves on to another society, the Longshan:

> Slightly later and slightly to the northeast, a more sophisticated Neolithic culture, the Longshan, grew up. The people of the Longshan made their pottery on wheels, whereas the Yanshao had coiled or molded their pots by hand. The Longshan people domesticated sheep and cattle, which were not seen in Yanshao sites. Longshan graves were dug under their own homes, while the Yanshao had buried their dead in graveyards far from their villages. Sometimes Longshan funeral urns were cemented into foundation walls, suggesting ancestor worship.[1]

The second-level point in this passage is the main idea—that the Longshan were an early Chinese people who were more sophisticated than the Yanshao. Third-level points support this idea: that the Longshan made pottery on wheels, that they domesticated sheep and cattle, and that they dug graves under their own houses (unlike the previous Yanshao people). In studying this paragraph, you should note all of these points.

As you identify these points, you should mark them for future reference. You can do this in several ways. Some professors recommend underlining (or highlighting) and making notes in the margins. In the author's opinion, the quickest and most flexible method is underlining or surrounding material with brackets using pencil. Pencil allows you to change your marks if your idea of what is important changes as you go back over the material. On the other hand, many historians advocate writing notes or summaries for each section, either by hand or on a computer, and then combining the notes on all the materials into one master set. Sometimes a combination of techniques will prove useful. Whatever method you choose, remember that effective studying requires more than simply reading, or even rereading, material. You must indicate the important points for study and then learn them thoroughly.

2. Use Your Memory Effectively

Although there are many reasons for studying history—understanding the past, interpreting it, and perceiving how historical developments are related to the present—in most courses students must commit a significant amount of information to memory and employ it effectively on tests. In doing so, it is helpful to know how the memory works. Basically, it consists of three parts: sensory, short-term, and long-term memory.

The first, the sensory memory, registers impressions conveyed by the senses. If, for example, you are driving down a street and hear a car horn honk, the sensory memory registers that sound—as well as everything else your senses perceive: a child shouting, the brake lights of a car ahead, the smell of newly mown grass wafting through the window. It holds most of these impressions for only a very short time—a fraction of a second to a few seconds, at the longest. Unless you do something to retain them, the impressions rapidly disappear. If they did not—if your memory held all sensations for long periods—you would be unable to concentrate on the important things.

If, on the other hand, you pay attention to a sensation, it moves to your short-term memory. The short-term memory, however, holds only a few items. The rule of thumb is seven plus or minus two—in other words, five to nine. And it retains them only a short time. Unless you do something to preserve them, items in short-term memory likewise fade quickly away—within seconds, in fact. In brief, both the sensory and short-term memories hold only small amounts of information and for only a short time.

To remember more information and remember it longer, you must transfer it to your long-term memory. Such a transfer requires specific, deliberate action. You cannot do so merely by reading or listening. Here are the most important techniques for transferring information to long-term memory:

- **Process the material.** Such processing involves making it your own, integrating it into your thinking. You can do this in several ways. First, you can reorganize it for yourself. If chronological order is important (as it often is), you can create your own chronologies. If you find cause-and-effect relationships, you can make charts that show these relationships. If items are related to each other hierarchically, you can create outlines that show the hierarchies. Second, you can connect the material to what you already know. This technique is effective because we remember best what relates to us most. Third, you can think critically about it. Analyze developments, ideas, and historical characters; compare them to others you are studying; examine the logic of arguments or developments; and evaluate what you study, making your own judgments about it.

- **Spread your study over time.** Divide it into a series of one- or two-hour sessions, and extend it over several days, rather than staging an exhausting all-night marathon. Also, break up your study sessions. Study a section of a chapter, then stop and get a drink of water, or do something else. If you are prone to boredom, this technique will help prevent it.
- **Practice "overlearning."** This means learning more thoroughly than you think necessary. Research has shown that it is extremely effective, and even if you think your time is in short supply, you should plan to study more than you might think you need to (see the section on time management below).
- **Review.** Drill yourself over knowledge you want to remember. You may already be use to doing this if, for example, you have used flash cards to memorize Spanish vocabulary words or math formulas. In your history class you can use this technique to remember the policies of Thomas Jefferson's administration, the criticisms of Ronald Reagan's policies, or the Four Noble Truths of Buddhism. In doing so, you are practicing retrieving information from your long-term memory, and such practice will help you retrieve it during tests.

3. Manage Your Time

Efficient time management is a proverbial secret of success. College classes are no exception. No matter how smart you are, doing anything—studying a textbook, reading a book, writing a paper—takes a certain amount of time; there are no shortcuts. For students, studies show, one of the keys to success is "seat time," the amount of time spent in a seat—studying. Research shows that most students, especially in their first two years of college or university, spend far too little time studying. So the first rule for success in a history (or any other) class is this: Put in enough time. How much? You have probably heard the old rule of thumb: two hours outside of class for every hour in class. You may discover that you do not need that much, but at the beginning of a course, do not underestimate the necessary study time.

Second, put your study time on a schedule. Block out specific times in your planner or calendar, and keep those appointments with yourself. Also, plan to study when you are naturally alert. If you are a morning person, for example, do not study history the last thing at night.

TEXTBOOKS

In studying a textbook, it is not enough simply to read, or even to reread. You have to study. But for many students, effective textbook studying does not come naturally. So what works? Here are proven techniques:

1. Survey the Material Before You Read it

Before beginning any trip, it is a good idea to know where you are going and how you are going to get there. The same principle applies to studying. Do not just sit down with a highlighter and start in. Before you begin reading, look over the material. Orient yourself. Ask yourself: What is the material about? How is it organized? How is it likely to fit in with other readings in the course? How does it correspond to what I already know? What is the author trying to do? Is he or she trying to provide facts, for example, or to describe debates in the subject, or to do something else entirely? What are the main points likely to be?

FOCUS questions

- WHY DID the world's population rise in the eighteenth century?
- WHY DID rising population stimulate economic activity in parts of Europe?
- WHY WAS China's position as the world's richest economy threatened in the eighteenth century?
- HOW DID British exploitation affect India's economy?
- HOW DID Imperial expansion stimulate economic activity?

Many textbooks provide features to help in previewing a chapter. Most have expanded tables of contents at the beginning of the book, which show not just the chapter but the subdivisions within them. In the chapters themselves, most textbooks also use subheadings to indicate these subdivisions. Some textbooks also have features at the beginning of chapters to help students focus on important points (such as the "Focus Questions" shown in the photo). You can also use objectives, which instructors often make available, or those provided by textbook publishers; these are usually available either in a printed study guide or on the publisher's Web site.[2] In short, the more you know about the material before you begin your reading, the more effective it is likely to be.

2. Identify Important Points as You Read

As you read, identify important points for future study by marking your book or taking notes. The section "Look for the Important Points, Not Just the Facts," earlier in this chapter, discusses the kinds of points to note. The following selection, describing Abraham Lincoln's plan for Reconstruction following the American Civil War, provides an example of how such points typically appear in history textbooks. The important points are underlined.

When the Civil War ended in 1865, no acceptable blueprint existed for reconstituting the Union. President Lincoln believed that, at heart, a majority of white Southerners were Unionists and that they could and should undertake the task of reconstruction. He favored a conciliatory policy toward the South in order, as he put it in one of his last letters, "to restore the Union, so as to make it . . . a Union of hearts and hands as well as of States." He counted on the loyalists to be fair with respect to the rights of the former slaves.

By late 1863, Union military victories had convinced President Lincoln of the need to fashion a plan for the reconstruction of the South . . . . Lincoln based his reconstruction program on bringing the seceded states back into the Union as quickly as possible. He was determined to respect private property (except in the case of slave property), and he opposed imposing harsh punishment for rebellion. His Proclamation of Amnesty and Reconstruction of December 1863 offered "full pardon" and the restoration of property, not including slaves, to white Southerners willing to swear an oath of allegiance to the United States and its laws, including the Emancipation Proclamation. Prominent Confederate military and civil leaders were excluded from Lincoln's offer, though he indicated that he would freely pardon them.

The president also proposed that when the number of any Confederate state's voters who took the oath of allegiance reached 10 percent of the number who had voted in the election of 1860, this group could establish a state government that Lincoln would recognize as legitimate. Fundamental to this Ten Percent Plan was acceptance by the reconstructed governments of the abolition of slavery. Lincoln's plan was designed less as a blueprint for Reconstruction than as a way to shorten the war and gain white people's support for emancipation. It angered those Republicans—known as Radical Republicans—who advocated not only equal rights for the freedmen [former slaves] but a tougher stance toward the white South. As a result, when Arkansas and Louisiana met the president's requirements for reentry into the Union, Congress refused to seat their representatives.[3]

As you can see, the main purpose of these three paragraphs is to describe Lincoln's Reconstruction policies. The important points, which you should note for study, include the conciliatory character of Lincoln's plan and his general goals, which were to bring the former Confederate states back into the Union as quickly as possible, to respect private property, and to avoid harsh punishment. You should also note the key features of the plan: full pardon and restoration of private property to all former Confederates who swore allegiance to the Union and its laws (including the Emancipation Proclamation, which abolished slavery); exclusion of high Confederate officials; and full restoration of self-government when 10 percent of eligible voters took a loyalty oath. You should also note the authors' comment that Lincoln's plan was based on acceptance of the abolition of slavery. And, finally, you should note the opposition the plan aroused among Radical Republications.

The density of important facts varies from book to book. Some authors pack them in tightly and surround them with very little other material. Others write in a looser style and include fewer important points per page or paragraph. Obviously, you should adjust your study to the style of the book.

As you study, avoid highlighting all or most of a page. The goal is to identify points to remember—to separate them from the mass of other material for study. Students who highlight an entire page have not distinguished anything from anything else; they have simply colored the page. Also, if you underline or highlight, try to limit your marks to the most important words rather than whole sentences. Notice, for example, how the excerpt above is marked. The marks are restricted to crucial words; all other phraseology is left unmarked.

What about dates, a subject more confused in the public mind than almost any other related to history? Although every student should understand and remember the basic chronology, such understanding does not mean memorizing every date in the book. Instead, you need to know the following types of dates. First, when did important events take place? Students studying China, for example, should remember that the Ming Dynasty came to power during the 1300s. Anyone studying the history of early modern Europe must know that the Protestant Reformation took place in the 1500s. Those studying modern Europe should remember that Napoleon was in power during the first fifteen years of the 1800s. Students of American history should remember that George Washington was president during the first half of the 1790s and that the Civil War was fought in the first half of the 1860s.

Second, what was the order of important events? In U.S. history, for example, students should know that George Washington was president before John Adams and that Adams was president before Thomas Jefferson. Those studying the U.S. Civil War should probably remember that Abraham Lincoln was elected president in November 1860 and also that the states of the Deep South passed secession ordinances between his election and his inauguration (when he actually became president) in March of the following year, 1861. In general, however, students do not have to remember the exact dates of each event. Every instructor, of course, teaches differently to some extent, so you should do your best to determine what sorts of dates she or he wants you to remember and in how much detail.

3. Use Effective Techniques to Learn the Material

Once you have distinguished the important points, you then have to learn them, to commit them to memory. To fix material in your memory, follow the principles described in the section on memory earlier in this chapter. One technique is to process the material. In doing this, you may, for instance, want to create a chronology or time line. Here is an example, in this case a chronology of Reconstruction:

MAJOR EVENTS OF RECONSTRUCTION

- Abraham Lincoln proposes his reconstruction plan (December 1863).
- Wade-Davis Bill passed by Congress; pocket-vetoed by Lincoln (1864).
- Lee surrenders, ending Civil War (April 1865).
- Lincoln assassinated; Andrew Johnson becomes president (April 1865).
- Thirteenth Amendment, abolishing slavery, ratified (December 1865).
- Congressional elections: Johnson campaigns against Republicans; Republicans win two-thirds majority in both houses of Congress (Fall 1866).
- House impeaches Johnson. Senate narrowly fails to remove him from office (1868).
- Ulysses S. Grant elected president (Fall 1868).
- Violence by Ku Klux Klan and other groups. Conservative Democrats regain control of former Confederate states (1869–1877).
- Hayes elected president. Removes federal troops from South; Reconstruction ends (1877).

Notice that this chronology lists events in order but does not give exact dates unless they are essential. Also, important words are underlined for ease of reference. When you create a chronology, however, you may use other formats and even include other events. In short, your chronology should be distinctively your own.

You can also create other kinds of charts, tables, and lists. Here, for example, is a table showing the main Reconstruction plans:

Reconstruction Plans

Plan	Provisions	Date	Results
Lincoln's Plan	When 10% of eligible voters took oath of loyalty, state could hold elections and rejoin Union.	1863	Congress refused to seat Representatives and Senators.
Wade-Davis Bill	50% of white men to take loyalty oath. Black civil rights guaranteed.	1864	Lincoln pocket-vetoed it.
Johnson's Plan	White southerners would take loyalty oath. Wealthy and former prominent Confederates excluded unless they received pardons. Informally told states to abolish slavery, repudiate Confederate debt.	1865	State governments formed. Congress refuses to seat newly elected Senators and Representatives.
First Reconstruction Act	Former Confederate states put under military control. Loyalty oaths. States required to guarantee African-American voting rights, ratify Fourteenth Amendment.	1867	Put into effect.

Another effective technique is relating the material you are studying to what you already know. In Reconstruction, for example, the Ku Klux Klan and other terrorist organizations played an important role. You could, therefore, link your current knowledge of the Ku Klux Klan—a violent, racist organization whose members sometimes wear robes and masks—to the fact that it was founded during Reconstruction and used violence to help conservative white Democrats take control of Southern states away from Reconstruction governments.

A third study technique is to employ critical thinking as an aid to memory. One type of critical thinking is analysis—taking phenomena apart and looking at their parts. In studying Reconstruction, you might, for instance, analyze the Radical Republicans. What, you might ask, were their main ideas, and what were the assumptions behind them? Another form of critical thinking is evaluation, which in history involves assessing historical policies, characters, and developments. In evaluating Reconstruction you could consider which aspects were successes and which were failures. In doing so, you might create a scorecard like this:

EVALUATING RECONSTRUCTION: SUCCESSES AND FAILURES

Successes

- Abolished slavery
- Created Constitutional guarantees of African-American civil and voting rights.
- Restored former Confederate states to Union.

Failures

- Did not give former slaves economic security in the form of land ownership.
- Did not provide African-Americans with social and political equality.

Another type of critical thinking involves comparing historical developments to current events. You could, for example, consider similarities between developments during Reconstruction and today. One other learning technique is examining how historical events are related to you. In studying Reconstruction, for instance, you could ask yourself what you could learn from it. How might you as a citizen and voter avoid the mistakes of that period?

4. Review

The final step in studying is review. Go over your notes (or your markings), quizzing yourself to see if you can remember them. When you remember a point, you can put a check mark by it in pencil. Then you can review items you did not remember the first time around. Go over material often, especially before quizzes, class discussions, and tests.

LECTURES

Since lectures are an important part of most history courses, you need to take good notes and use them effectively. Before taking notes, however, even before going to class, you should study the assigned reading. The background it provides is often crucial for fully understanding lectures, especially since many are not simply recitations of facts but commentary, giving the instructor's own interpretation. Then, when attending a lecture, observe the following principles:

Look for the Important Points

As you take notes, your goal should be to summarize the main points along with the lecturer's reasoning and the supporting evidence. In deciding what to write down in your notes, use any aids the lecturer provides. These may include outlines on a board, overhead transparencies, or PowerPoint slides. Also, listen for verbal cues, such as pauses, more emphatic tones of voice, or enumerations, such as "first," "second," or "third."

Do not think of yourself as a human dictation machine. Your role is to listen intelligently and interpret the material for future use. Do not, therefore, try to write everything down or to write it down word for word. At the same time, however, avoid the opposite pitfall, which some students fall into in their first year of college, of taking too few notes. If in doubt about whether something is important, err on the side of caution, and write it down.

In taking notes, make sure you understand the point the lecturer is making. Is he or she, for instance, saying that one event is more important than another? If so, be sure to indicate that—do not just put down the facts about both events. Perhaps the professor is describing arguments made by historians. In that case, say so; don't simply report the arguments as facts.

Take Effective Notes

As you take notes, try to show the relationship of various points to each other. Using an outline format can be useful because it forces you to indicate the logical relationship of points to each other. You can also use charts, arrows, and other devices to indicate relationships.

Take notes efficiently. Writing complete sentences is usually a waste of time. Abbreviate wherever possible, but be sure to use only abbreviations you will understand later. You can take notes using different writing instruments and various sizes of paper. Most people seem to prefer 8.5"× 11" paper (even in Europe, where a similar size is called A7), but you can try other sizes. Pens are usually more legible than pencils. Also, leave wide margins on both sides of the page so that you can write notes in them as you study. Here is an example of one page of lecture notes on a world history lecture about World War I:

WORLD HISTORY II   Page 1

April 10

World War I

   I. Origins

       A. Competition for markets, colonies

          1. All major European countries competing for colonies, raw materials, markets in late nineteenth century.

                                        (*continued*)

2. German unification and growth of German economy
made it a competitor of France, Britain.

B. Creation of Franco-Russian alliance.

1. Until 1891 Bismarck (German chancellor) had been careful to keep alliance w/ both Russia & Austro-Hungary.

2. New Kaiser, Wilhelm II, dismissed Bismarck. Failed to renew alliance with Russia.

3. Russia then formed alliance with France.

a. Led to possibility of two-front war for Germany.

C. Naval competition

1. 1890s Germany began creation of large fleet.

2. Britain felt threatened, responded by

a. Building even larger fleet.

b. Forming alliance w/France.

Notice the aspects of good note-taking this page illustrates. First, the student has clearly indicated the name of the course, the date of the lecture, and the page number of the notes for this lecture. (What is shown above is just the first page of notes on the lecture.) That information is important in case this page gets separated from the rest of the notes. The student has also left wide margins on both sides of the page. The notes are in outline form. Roman numeral I, for example, tells us that what follows will be a discussion of the origins (or causes) of the war. Each capital letter (A, B, and C) is used for a cause of the war discussed by the lecturer. The Arabic numerals (1, 2, 3, etc.) are used for points that provide additional information. In one instance, under C.2., small letters are used to enumerate Britain's response to the German threat.

This lecture, like many others, is not merely a description of facts. In naming certain factors as the origins of the war, the lecturer is offering an interpretation. Other historians might disagree and list other factors.

Some note-taking methods call for leaving unusually large margins on one side of the page, allowing room to write comments when you study. Another calls for dividing the pages down the middle, writing lecture notes on one side and notes from the textbook on the other. You can experiment to see how these methods work for you.

Whatever method you use, you should keep your notes in a form that allows you to add or remove material. Notes are not sacred writings to preserve for all time in their original form. A loose-leaf binder is helpful. It will allow you to make new copies of pages, remove old ones, and add new material.

If your professor permits, you might try a laptop computer. You can probably type faster than you can write by hand. Other options include tablet computers or PDAs, with or without plug-in keyboards. Any device for putting notes in computerized format will enable you to move your notes around and reorganize them more easily than if they were written by hand.

What about tape recording instead of note taking? While this technique may be good for some purposes, like getting an interviewee's exact words, it is usually inefficient for lectures. Of course, if you have difficulty understanding spoken English or have some condition that prevents you from writing, taping may be an alternative. But most of the time, it is a very distant second best. The reason is simple: When you take notes, you sort through what you hear, looking for important points and, in the process, discard the unimportant things that every speaker says. In addition, you organize the information as you write—an important step in remembering. If you simply tape a lecture, you have to listen to the whole thing and then go through those processes all over again.

Study Your Notes Efficiently

Go over your notes as soon as possible after class. Make sure that you understand them. With the lecture reasonably fresh in your mind, you can correct anything unclear. Sometimes you may want to clarify your notes by adding explanations. You may also find it useful to insert your own headings to indicate the subjects of sections. At either this stage or later, you can call attention to important points by notes in the margin, underlining, stars, or other marks. At some point, it is a good idea to combine your lecture notes with notes from various readings. Putting the notes from all the materials together and indicating their relationship will enrich your understanding and help you remember the material.

In doing this, you will have already begun the process of learning the material and, in psychological terms, putting it into your long-term memory. You should now continue the process. Use the techniques described in the section "Use Your Memory Effectively." Remember the principle of "overlearning," and study more than you think is necessary.

MAPS

Because historical events happen in specific geographic locations, maps are important tools for understanding them. Almost all history books contain maps, and many instructors expect their students to use and understand them. Sometimes they even assign map exercises or require specific map knowledge on tests.

Most maps have tools for interpretation. These include a title, a caption, a legend, (which tells you the meaning of the specific marks), and a scale (which shows the distances in the map). The map below, from the U. S. history textbook *Out of Many*, illustrates most of these features (it does not include a caption).

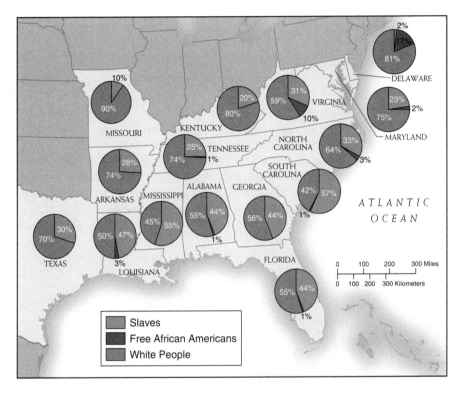

Population Patterns in the South, 1850. A typical map in a U.S. history textbook.

The title indicates the subject of the map: "Population Patterns in the South, 1850." As you can see, the population patterns are the percentages of whites, free African-Americans, and slaves. A pie chart indicates the percentage of each of these groups in each state. The legend shows the shading used within the charts for each of these groups. A scale shows the relative distances on the map.

In studying this, or any other, map, you should ask two questions: First, what facts does it show? Second, what is the significance of these facts? In this map the facts are the percentage of each group (whites, free African-Americans, and slaves) in the population of the each Southern state shortly before the Civil War.

What is the significance of these facts? Sometimes authors spell out the significance, either in the caption or in the text of the book. In other cases, they let the readers figure it out. In this map one of the most striking facts is the high percentage of slaves in the Lower South of South Carolina, Georgia, Florida, Alabama, Mississippi, and Louisiana. In all of these states, slaves made up more than 40 percent of the population; in two of them, South Carolina and Mississippi, they comprised a majority. What significance might this fact have? It might suggest that the large numbers of slaves in the Lower South states frightened white Southerners. And, in fact, they did.

It might also suggest that large plantations with big slave populations were more important in the Lower South states than in those in the Upper South, and they were. Notice the much lower percentages of slaves in Upper South states. The highest proportion in any of them was only 33 percent (in North Carolina); in the others it was even smaller. These lower slave percentages suggest that the Upper South had proportionately fewer large plantations and more small and medium-size farms. Knowing this, you might also deduce that the differences in farm size and slaveholding resulted in large part from different kinds of agriculture practiced in the Upper South, especially the crops grown. That would also be correct. In the Lower South conditions favored cotton cultivation, which was most profitable when cultivated by large numbers of slaves. This, in turn, meant large plantations. The Upper South, on the other hand, was generally less conducive to cotton growing, and while some areas produced tobacco or other cash crops that were suited to cultivation by large numbers of slaves, many farmers instead practiced a mixed agriculture, often featuring the growing of grain and raising of livestock, which was less economically suited to large slave work forces.

PRIMARY-SOURCE DOCUMENTS

Primary-source documents—those written contemporaneously by observers or participants—are the raw material of history. They may be assigned as reading or as preparation for a writing assignment. Whatever the case, you should be able to answer the following questions about any document you study:

1. Who wrote it, and to whom?
2. When was it written?
3. What are the main points?
4. What does it reveal about the characters and historical period under study?

Answering the first two questions is usually simple, requiring only a perusal of an introductory note. Answering the others requires an examination of the document.

Here is a typical document that might be assigned in a world or Asian history course, a message from the Chinese emperor Qian Long, written in

1793 to King George III of Great Britain in response to a British proposal for permanent diplomatic representation and expanded trade. At this point, Great Britain was the first nation in the world to have entered the industrial revolution. British industries had begun to use steam engines, to employ mass production, and to produce large quantities of iron in factories. Already one of the world's greatest military powers, Britain was using its industrial prowess to modernize its army and navy. A mere fifty years later, the British, armed with modern weapons, would decisively defeat China and force it to accept humiliating terms of surrender. With these facts in mind, notice what the Chinese emperor writes to George III:

> You, O King, live beyond the confines of many seas[;] nevertheless, impelled by your humble desire to partake of the benefits of our civilisation, you have dispatched a mission respectfully bearing your memorial. Your Envoy has crossed the seas and paid his respects at my Court on the anniversary of my birthday. To show your devotion, you have also sent offerings of your country's produce.
>
> I have perused your memorial: The earnest terms in which it is couched reveal a respectful humility on your part, which is highly praiseworthy. In consideration of the fact that your Ambassador and his deputy have come a long way with your memorial and tribute, I have shown them high favour and have allowed them to be introduced into my presence. To manifest my indulgence, I have entertained them at a banquet and made them numerous gifts. I have also caused presents to be forwarded to the Naval Commander and six hundred of his officers and men, although they did not come to Peking, so that they too may share in my all-embracing kindness.
>
> As to your entreaty to send one of your nationals to be accredited to my Celestial Court and to be in control of your country's trade with China, this request is contrary to all usage of my dynasty and cannot possibly be entertained.[4]

In reading this document, you could find answers to the first two questions—the writer and the time of writing—in the introductory material: The author is the Chinese emperor Qian Long, who wrote it to King George III at the end of the eighteenth century (1793). An examination of the document itself reveals the main point: The emperor will not accept British diplomatic representatives in China. What does the message reveal about the characters and historical period under study? First, it shows the emperor's sense of complete superiority over the British and all other foreigners. He had no notion whatsoever that Britain was undergoing an industrial revolution that in a few years would enable it to inflict a humiliating defeat on China.

In reading such a document, you should take notes on important information and organize them in a format easily accessible for future review. Here is an example:

WORLD HISTORY

Notes on Primary-Source Document

Document:
Message from Chinese emperor Qian Long, to King George III of
Great Britain

Author:
Qian Long, Chinese emperor

When Written
1793

Main Points
Will not allow permanent British representative.

What Document Reveals:
1. Chinese emperor has sense of complete superiority over
   British.
2. Emperor has no idea that industrialization would soon make
   Britain and other Western countries superior to China.

You can write such notes by hand or with a computer (preferably). Once
you have taken notes, you should study them using the techniques of efficient learning described earlier in this chapter.

Students sometimes find the language in documents difficult. In such
cases, you can begin with a modern dictionary; most provide current definitions of words and information about their origins. If puzzled, however, by
words employed in ways seemingly different from modern usage, you can
consult the *Oxford English Dictionary*, a monumental work recording the use
of all English words throughout history. It is available in most libraries and on
the Internet, by subscription. If you have to look up a lot of words, you may
find working with other students helpful.

INTERPRETIVE ESSAYS AND BOOKS

You may also be assigned to read interpretive essays or books. Such assignments
may include journal articles, chapters in anthologies ("readers"), or even books,
usually called monographs. While professors sometimes assign such reading
mainly to provide students with information, in many cases the goal is to introduce them to interpretations. If possible, find out the purpose from your professor.

Whatever the purpose, you should, at a minimum, determine the author's thesis and the supporting evidence. If, for example, an article discusses the U.S. decision to drop atomic bombs on Hiroshima and Nagasaki at the end of World War II, the author may argue that the decision was unjustified—or justified—depending on the article. Sometimes an author states the thesis in so many words, often in the introduction. Frequently, an author will also restate the thesis in the conclusion. Sometimes, however, the thesis will be merely implied. Whatever the case, you should identify the thesis and remember it.

In books written by scholars, the thesis often appears in a preface, where the author also discuss other scholarship on the subject. Rather than ignoring this introductory material, you should read it carefully. In addition, a historian will often restate the thesis and discuss the book's significance in the final chapter. You may, therefore, want to read the preface and conclusion before reading the body of the book. In both books and articles, you should also, of course, note and remember the supporting evidence.

Often, instructors expect students not only to understand but to evaluate readings. In doing so, you should consider the following questions:

• When was the essay or book written?
• How does its argument compare with other things written on the subject?
• Is the evidence persuasive?
• How does the book's argument compare with your own thinking?

The date of publication is important. An article discussing slavery written in 2001 will probably differ in at least some respects from one written in 1960, because historians' views on the subject have changed. Something written more recently is not necessarily correct just because it is newer. But you should understand that historical thinking changes over time, because of research, scholarly reexamination of previous work, and historians' response to changing circumstances in society and politics. You should also compare the interpretation with those of your textbook and lectures. Does it agree or disagree? In what respects? If you have read other articles on the subject, compare the current reading with them. The question, Is the evidence persuasive? should not be answered simply yes or no. You should be able to give reasons for your answer. Finally, ask yourself, How does this argument fit into my own thinking? Do you agree? Disagree? In what ways? Why? The ultimate purpose of studying history is to enable you to form independent judgments.

As you study, it is useful to keep notes in a form that you can study. Here is an example:

Author and Article	Thesis	Supporting Arguments

You can write such notes by hand, but a computer offers many advantages. As you study, combine the notes on interpretive readings with those on other materials in the course, including the lectures and textbooks. Before tests, study them, using the techniques of efficient learning.

HISTORICAL NOVELS AND OTHER FICTION

Professors assign fiction for several reasons: to dramatize a historical period, to personalize characters, to bring a period to life, or perhaps to give students an exercise in evaluating how a piece of fiction compares with current historical knowledge of the subject. In studying historical fiction, it is important to realize the assignment is not recreational reading. Try to determine what your instructor wants you to get out of the material. Many will make detailed assignments, or at least describe what they are looking for. If they do, pay careful attention and use their instructions as a guide. If your professor gives you no other guidance, be able to answer at least the following questions:

1. How does the work of fiction portray the period and the events it describes?
2. How does this portrayal compare to what you have learned from other material in the course—your textbook, lectures, other sources of information?
3. Based on those materials, to what extent is the portrayal accurate?
4. What does it add to your understanding of the period it covers?

As in the study of other material, it is useful to make notes on historical fiction, combine them with notes on other assignments, study them using the techniques of efficient learning, and review them in preparation for tests.

PAINTINGS, PHOTOGRAPHS, AND OTHER GRAPHIC MATERIAL

Professors sometimes ask their students to study historical paintings, drawings, and photographs. You should view these both as sources of information and as interpretations. The drawing below shows how graphic materials can provide historical information. It portrays a spinning jenny, a machine that turned fiber into thread. This device was one of the most important inventions in the early industrial revolution, and the drawing shows, among other things, its remarkable simplicity.

A spinning jenny

Besides presenting information, graphic materials often interpret the material they portray. An example is Francisco de Goya's painting the *Execution of the Defenders of Madrid, 3rd May, 1808*. It shows French troops during the Napoleonic wars shooting members of the Spanish resistance during the French invasion of Spain. In his arresting depiction of the brutality of the execution, Goya is clearly interpreting the event, and that interpretation is important.

Although assignments may vary, the following questions will guide you in studying artwork assigned in a history course:

1. Who created the work?
2. When was it created?

The "Execution of the Defenders of Madrid, 3rd May, 1808" painted by Francisco de Goya.

   3. What does it show?
   4. What interpretation does it make?
   5. What insight does it give into the period you are studying?

In the case of the Goya painting, you might make the following notes:

PAINTING: GOYA'S *EXECUTION OF THE DEFENDERS OF MADRID, 3RD MAY, 1808*

Creator	Francisco de Goya
When created	1814
Shows	French troops executing Spanish resistance fighters
Interpretation	Brutality, cruelty of French troops, French invasion
Insights into period	Human face of Napoleonic wars, nationalism aroused in Europe

---

Steamboats tied up along the Mississippi River.

Like other graphic materials, photographs, too, may provide factual information. For example, the picture above showing steamboats tied up along a Mississippi River bank reveals what these boats looked like.

On the other hand, despite the widespread belief that photographs simply show facts, photographers may use them to convey powerful interpretations. Consider, for example, this haunting photograph (next page) from Depression-era America taken by Russell Lee in 1936. The interpretation seems obvious: The Depression is a human catastrophe, and something must be done about it.

Even less emotional photographs, however, may present interpretations. Look, for example, at the next photograph, which on the surface, simply shows people lining up for food. What interpretation, however, might the photographer intend?

Sometimes photographs can actually lie. The photographs on page 45 reveal one of the most notorious examples in recent history. Both show Vladimir Ilyich Lenin, the leader of the Bolshevik revolution in the Soviet Union, speaking to troops in 1920. The photograph on the top is the original. When it was taken, Leon Trotsky, Lenin's second in command and a leader of the revolution, occupied a prominent place in the picture. In the original photo, on the top, he is sitting just to the right and below the speaker, Lenin, facing sideways. After Lenin's death, however, Josef Stalin, another Bolshevik leader, engaged in a

Christmas dinner in home of Earl Pauley near Smithfield, Iowa, 1936. Dinner consisted of potatoes, cabbage, and pie. Photograph by Russell Lee.

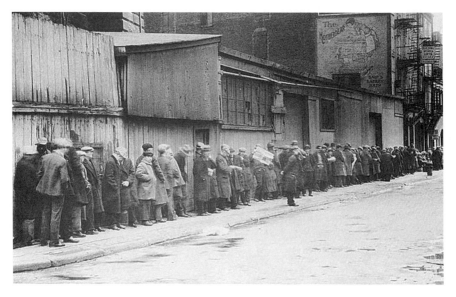

Breadline at McCauley Water Street Mission under Brooklyn Bridge, New York, during the Great Depression.

The original photo on the top, showing Trotsky, and doctored photo below, with Trotsky removed.

bitter power struggle with Trotsky. After winning, he banished Trotsky from the Soviet Union and eventually had him assassinated in Mexico. Under Stalin, Soviet officials, in their desire to destroy evidence of Trotsky's previous position with Lenin and during the Bolshevik revolution, went so far as actually to remove his image from the official version of the photograph—the one on the bottom. In this photograph you can see that Trotsky is gone. This brazen tampering shows dramatically how photographs can be subject to alteration. Such manipulation is even easier in the age of computers.

In studying photographs, you should put the same type of information in your notes as you do for other artworks. Here is an example of notes on the photograph of the children's Depression Christmas dinner:

Title of photograph	Christmas dinner in home of Earl Pauley near Smithfield, Iowa, 1936
Creator	Russell Lee
When created	1936 (during Depression)
Shows	Four children eating, Christmas dinner, according to title. No chairs, Food appears to be extremely simple. House walls unfinished.
Interpretation	Children apparently in abject poverty. Conditions pathetic. Something should be done about this.
Insight into period	Horrifying poverty evidently common in Great Depression. Some photographers trying to express their outrage.

You should, of course, combine your notes on photographs with those on other materials and study them before discussions and tests.

FILMS AND VIDEOTAPES

Films and videotapes used in history classes usually fall into two basic types: nonfiction, which includes documentary footage and commentaries, like those in the public television series *The American Experience*; and feature films, fictional treatment of historical periods or events, like *Glory*, the story of a black regiment in the American Civil War. Since film use in history courses varies, try to ascertain how your instructor wants you to view the film. In general, however, you should observe the following guidelines.

Treat educational or other factual films and videotapes as you would a lecture. Take notes on the major points of fact and interpretation. Compare them with your lecture and reading notes. Use effective means of learning, and review before tests.

Scene from the film *Glory*.

For fictional films, like *Glory*, take notes that enable you to make the kind of analysis you would construct for a piece of historical fiction. These notes should enable you to answer the following questions:

1. How does the film portray the period and events it describes?
2. How does the film's portrayal compare to what you have learned from other materials in the course?
3. Based on those materials, to what extent is the film accurate?
4. What does the film add to your understanding of the period it covers?

Accuracy is often an issue in films dealing with historical events. Frequently, a film's version of the facts is suspect. It is therefore important to compare the film to your textbook or other authoritative sources.

Sometimes films use actual footage of historical events. The makers of *Forest Gump*, for instance, inserted images of Tom Hanks in the role of Gump into actual news footage of historical events, making it appear that Gump was there. The filmmakers do not seem to have been attempting any deception; any halfway intelligent viewer would understand that the movie was fiction and that Gump was not actually there. More controversial is Oliver Stone's movie *JFK*, in which the distinction between historical images and those produced by Stone are sometimes unclear. In any case, the ease with which a filmmaker can blur the distinction between historical and fictional images should alert the viewer to the possibilities of deception in films. Pictures, it turns out, can lie—and have done so. In viewing history films, therefore, be alert for accuracy.

Films also interpret the past, and their interpretations can be highly problematic. A classic example is *The Triumph of the Will*, a film about a Nazi party rally in Nuremburg, Germany, made by the German filmmaker Leni Riefenstahl. You may view this film in a world history or Western civilization class. It shows scene after scene of young Nazis, healthy, determined, exhibiting complete order and unanimity. It then shows Hitler arriving by airplane (an example of modern technology in the 1930s) like a super-human being, revealing himself to the immense but completely disciplined masses awaiting him on the ground.

In U.S. history, the film *The Birth of a Nation* is similarly problematic and is often shown for many of the same reasons. One of the classic early films, it portrays the American South after the Civil War being ravaged by ignorant, animalistic African-Americans and corrupt white "carpetbaggers." Salvation, according to the movie, came through the Ku Klux Klan, which helped restore power to the honest and benevolent white people of the South.

Although these are among the most famous (or infamous) films dealing with historical phenomena, all films present interpretations. As a history student, one of your tasks in viewing a film is to identify the interpretation. You can then compare it with those of other materials on the same subject. When you see a film as part of a history class, your instructor may make specific assignments, but if you do not receive such an assignment, you should, at the very least, take notes on the film in which you indicate the interpretation and the cinematic devices used to convey it.

As this chapter shows, studying history effectively requires the application of general principles to each type of assignment in your course. This means identifying the main points, both of fact and interpretation. You must then note them in a form in which you can study them. After that, you should process them intellectually to make them your own. At this point it is useful to combine the notes from different materials. Finally, before any test or other occasion where you will be graded, you must review the material thoroughly.

<hr>

QUICK REVIEW

- **General principles:** Look for important points, use effective memory techniques, and manage your time.
- **Textbooks:** Survey the material before reading it, identify the important points, use effective learning techniques, and review.
- **Lectures:** Put the important points in your notes and study them efficiently.
- **Maps:** Understand what the map is showing, and know the point (or points) the map is making.
- **Primary-source documents:** Know who wrote the document, when it was written, what the main points are, and what it tells you about the period, events, or personalities under discussion.
- **Interpretive essays and books:** Know the author's thesis and supporting arguments. Examine when the material was written, whether the evidence is persuasive, how the work compares with other writing on the subject, and how it fits into your own thinking.
- **Historical fiction:** Consider how the work portrays the historical period and events. Compare this to what you have learned from other sources.
- **Artwork, including photographs:** Look for what the work reveals about the period, the viewpoint of the work, and the possible manipulation of images.
- **Films and videotapes:** If nonfiction, take notes and study as you would for lectures. Study feature films as you would historical fiction, being alert to interpretation.

<hr>

NOTES

1. Howard Spodek, *The World's History*, Vol. 1: *Prehistory to 1500*, 3rd ed. (Upper Saddle River, NJ: Prentice Hall, 2006), 90.

2. For example, you can find objectives for Prentice Hall textbooks at http://vig.prenhall.com/catalog/academic/discipline/0,4094,2677,00.html, where you can log in to "History Central."

3. John Mack Faragher, Mari Jo Buhle, Daniel Czitrom, and Susan H. Armitage, *Out of Many: A History of the American People*, 4th ed. (Upper Saddle River, NJ: Prentice Hall, 2003), 501.

4. Harley Farnsworth MacNair, *Modern Chinese History, Selected Readings* (Shanghai: Commercial Press Ltd., 1923), 2–9.

CHAPTER 5

HOW TO PARTICIPATE EFFECTIVELY IN CLASS

AT A GLANCE

Discussions
- Participate regularly.
- Be informed.
- Think critically about the material.
- Be sensitive to other class members.

Class Presentations
- Organize your presentation.
- Prepare thoroughly.
- Use a conversational tone.

Group Projects
- Meet early to organize the work.
- Assign each person a specific task.
- Establish deadlines.
- Rehearse all presentations.

Many history classes require student participation, which frequently includes class discussions for which you receive grades, as well as oral presentations or group projects. This chapter discusses strategies for success in these activities.

DISCUSSIONS

Some courses contain formal discussion periods for which students receive grades; many instructors also encourage student questions and discussion in lecture sessions. For discussions, grading practices vary among instructors. Some have specific criteria; others have more general expectations. In your class, try to determine what your instructor expects. Listen carefully to what he or she says, and, if possible, ask for details and examples. Of course, if you receive written directions, read them carefully. Regardless of how much detail you get, most historians have certain common expectations. They want students to participate, to be informed about the material from the course, to think critically about the material, and to be sensitive to other participants in the discussion.

Participate

Unless the instructor tells you otherwise, be sure to participate at least once in every discussion. Many instructors want students to do this several times, so be prepared for that as well. In some cases, especially when the group is large, instructors frown on someone seeming to dominate the discussion; try to avoid any appearance of doing this. Depending on the characteristics of your group, you may have to walk a fine line between excessive silence and talking, but, in general, err on the side of participation.

Be Informed

Most instructors do not intend class discussions to be mere recreation; they want students to grapple intelligently with the material under discussion. In discussions, therefore, stick to the subject and demonstrate your knowledge of the course materials—lectures, textbooks, and any other readings assigned. Whenever possible, support your statements with specific evidence from the course. Not only should you be informed, you want to sound that way, too. To do so, you can cite specific course materials, by saying, for example, "As _____ [give the author's name] says . . . " Then mention the fact or interpretation.

Think Critically About the Material

In addition to familiarity with the facts, most instructors want students to think critically about the material. As often as possible, therefore, include thoughts as well as facts in your contributions. You may find it useful to employ certain types of critical thinking in discussions. These include analysis, in which you analyze, or take something apart. In a history class this could be a historical development or an idea. You might, for example, consider why a particular event took place or why a certain group behaved in certain ways. Another form of critical thought is comparison. You could examine, for example, how two groups were similar or different. If you were studying the revolutionary movements of 1848 in Europe, for example, you might compare the revolutionary groups in Paris with the Chartists in England. You can also consider how historical developments are similar or different. In a world history class, you might ask how feudalism in Japan was similar to or different from medieval European feudalism. Another technique is comparing a historical development to something in the present. In discussing the politics of the late-nineteenth-century United States, for example, you might ask yourself how the political parties of that period are different from or similar to those of today. In evaluation you make a judgment. In this type of thought you might ask whether a historian's argument is logical, or what the strengths and weaknesses of an argument were. Another kind of thinking is synthesis, in which you put several ideas together and, in doing so, come up with your own theory.

Be Sensitive to Other Class Members

Expectations of decorum vary from class to class, but in general you should observe some simple rules. First, stay on the subject. Sometimes it is easy to go off on tangents, especially when everyone seems to be having a good time, but discipline yourself. Second, as discussed earlier, avoid dominating the conversation. Third, when you disagree, do so politely. Fourth, refrain from simply parroting what other people say.

Doing all of these things may seem like a tall order. You can, however, prepare for discussions, and you should. Before class, go over the things likely to be discussed. If the instructor hands out a list of topics or questions in advance, so much the better. Make notes, including what you might say about certain questions, and take them to class.

PRESENTATIONS

In history classes, oral presentations can take several forms, among them book reviews, reports on research, and discussions of reading. The instructor's expectations of the students may also vary. As with any other assignment, you should try to learn as much as possible about the requirements in advance. Be sure to read anything in writing, like a syllabus or an instruction sheet. If you have questions, ask your instructor or teaching assistant. But whatever the specific requirements in your class, the following principles will help make your presentation successful.

Organize

Prepare your presentation thoroughly in advance. In general, you should organize it as you would an essay, with an introduction, a body, and a conclusion. The introduction should introduce the subject and suggest its significance; it should usually also include a thesis statement. In the body, make your main points, and support them. And, finally, of course, you will need a brief conclusion, where you suggest the importance of your subject.

Prepare

Prepare a class presentation as thoroughly as you would a written assignment. In delivering a presentation, you can choose one of several techniques: reading a written manuscript, memorizing and reciting a speech, talking from a memorized outline, speaking from notes, or making the whole thing up as you go along. Reading a speech has the advantage of allowing you to establish the exact wording in advance. When precise words are important—when they are matters of historic or legal significance—reading may be justified. U.S. presidents, for example, read inaugural and state-of-the-union addresses. But reading requires considerable skill and extensive practice, and most read speeches are deadly dull. Unless you are giving a historic address, therefore, avoid reading.

A second method is to write a speech and memorize it. This technique, again, has the advantage of allowing you to set down exact phraseology in advance. In addition, some people may think you are brilliant for being able to speak without notes; they sometimes admire preachers and professors who do this. But memorization is laborious and, frankly, too much work for most class presentations.

A third approach is to make notes and speak from them, a practice of many experienced speakers. For notes, 3" × 5" cards are a common preference. The late President Ronald Reagan, known as "the great communicator," often used this method (he once even used notes written on cards to greet a guest). For most class (and other) presentations, speaking from notes is the best method. It allows you to organize your thoughts carefully in advance, frees you from having to memorize large amounts of material, and facilitates a conversational style of speaking.

An alternative method is to make the notes part of a PowerPoint presentation and speak as they appear on the screen. This technique, of course, requires the necessary equipment, but many classrooms have it. Although PowerPoint is the norm in many businesses, it has detractors, and some major corporations have even banned it. Critics maintain that it tends to make presentations formulaic; it can also separate the speaker from the audience. If considering PowerPoint for a class presentation, weigh the pros and cons carefully and consult your instructor beforehand.

To prepare for any kind of oral presentation, begin with an outline; then review it carefully. If you plan to speak from notes, put the points from your outline into notes. You can write them on a single piece of paper or, as we have discussed, on cards. Both techniques have advantages and disadvantages. Cards are less conspicuous than larger pieces of paper, which is why many speakers use them. However, a single page shows you the entire talk at a glance and often increases a speaker's peace of mind. Notes should contain main points, not whole sentences. Sentences are hard to read, and you should usually avoid preparing exact phraseology in advance—unless you have some particularly fine wording you want to utter. If you do, memorize those particular bon mots. If you use PowerPoint, your main points will, of course, appear on slides, but you may want to supplement them with written notes. Regardless of the technique, rehearse your talk several times. Even if you plan to read it—especially if you plan to read it—go over it frequently.

Whenever possible, include illustrations: transparencies, slides, computer files, PowerPoint presentations, videotapes, or DVDs. If you use material from movies or TV programs, make it short and relevant. You can also use sound recordings containing spoken material, music, or other sounds from a variety of media: tape, DVDs, or MP3 files. Finally, anytime you use equipment, do a dry run, if possible.

Use a Conversational Tone

The high-flown formal oratory of Patrick Henry ("Give me liberty or give me death") and Daniel Webster is long out of date. Speak in a conversational tone. Even presidents do so nowadays. When talking to more than a few people or in a large room, you must, of course, project yourself: Speak a little more loudly and a little more emphatically, but still be natural.

GROUP PROJECTS

Many history classes require group projects. These can be rewarding but have potential pitfalls as well, as you may already have discovered. Here are some principles to help make group work effective:

Meet Early to Organize the Work

As soon as possible, get the whole group together and organize the work. Group work requires more organization than work by individuals, so it is important to organize the project thoroughly. Meet and do this early, so you will have the maximum amount of time. At the organizational meeting, discuss the work entailed and divide it into specific tasks. Each person in the group should write down all of this. Also, be sure that each person has each of the others' phone numbers and e-mail addresses.

Assign Each Person a Specific Task

As you probably know, one of the biggest pitfalls in group work is that often some people shirk and others do more than their share, often unwillingly. To counteract this tendency, assign each group member a task, requiring, of course, approximately the same amount of work. If possible, arrange for each member's name to be put on his or her part of the final product as well as the project as a whole. Some instructors give each member of the group the same grade; others give both individual and group grades. Even when there is only a group grade, publicly identifying the part done by each person will encourage responsibility.

Establish Deadlines Along with Meeting Times

At the first meeting, establish deadlines for each stage of the project. Deadlines for every phase work much better than a only single final deadline. Also, assign all group members deadlines for each phase of their tasks. Finally, schedule meetings for each deadline, so that the whole group makes sure that each member is meeting individual deadlines.

Rehearse Public Presentations

Many projects require public presentations. If that is the case with your project, be sure to rehearse as a group at least once. As any actor will tell you, rehearsal—frequent rehearsal—is the only way to put on a polished performance.

QUICK REVIEW

- **Discussions:** Participate regularly, be informed, think critically about the material, and be sensitive to other students.
- **Presentations:** Organize your material, prepare thoroughly, and use a conversational tone.
- **Groups:** Meet early to organize the work, assign each person a task, establish deadlines, and rehearse all presentations.

CHAPTER 6

SUCCESS WITH TESTS

AT A GLANCE

When Studying for Tests
- Concentrate on the important points.
- Combine information from different sources.
- Organize the material for yourself as you study.
- Prepare for the specific test.
- Spread your study over several sessions.

During the Test
- Plot a strategy before you begin.
- Use the principles of good English composition in written answers.
- Use the right strategy for each question.

Although the purpose of a history course is more than simply passing tests, in most classes exams are important, and most students want to deal with them as proficiently as possible. Studying, of course, should begin long before the test. But for the best results, prepare specifically for each test and use the most effective techniques in taking it.

STUDYING FOR TESTS

Concentrate on the Important Points

Studies of test-taking reveal an apparently strange fact: No matter what kind of exam you take, you do better if you have studied for an essay test. The reason, according to this research, is that we remember more easily if we see the whole picture, and essay questions require students to do that. Fortunately, this finding accords with the way history works, for historians are far more interested in ideas and interpretations than mere facts. As you review for a test, therefore, try to identify the major points—the important developments, ideas, and interpretations. Then organize the facts around these points. Often, your lecture notes, which should reflect your instructor's emphases, will help you identify these points; you may see others in the class readings.

Put Information from All the Course Materials Together

History instructors often use various kinds of materials: textbooks, lectures, documents, interpretive articles, other readings, and maps. Students are supposed to understand how each illuminates the developments in the course. In preparing for a test, study all of them rather than just the textbook or lecture notes; observe how each contributes to your understanding of historical developments. A good way to study these disparate materials is to review one theme or development at a time, comparing all the relevant materials.

In studying Reconstruction in a U.S. history course, for example, begin with your lecture notes. Try to determine your instructor's approach, the main emphases, the interpretations. Next, turn to the textbook; go over the relevant sections. If you have followed the techniques recommended by this book, you would already have put marks in your book or made notes to indicate important points. Review them. Then look over any documents or essays assigned, and review your notes on them. Finally, summarize, either mentally or on paper, what each of these sources says on the subject and how they fit together, or, perhaps, conflict. Carry out the same procedure for other major topics. Obviously, this process will entail serious work, but it will help you master the material.

Organize the Material for Yourself as You Study

As Chapter 4, "How to Study History," explains, you remember best if you organize material to fit your own way of thinking. Useful tools for such organization include chronologies and lists. You may have already constructed chronologies when you first studied the material. As you review, however, you might want to make new ones. Here, for example, is a chronology of the period between World Wars I and II that you might make in a world or European history course:

1918	World War I ends.
1923	Height of German inflation.
1923	Hitler attempts coup, arrested, goes to prison.
1924	Dawes Plan stabilizes German finances.
1929	Great Depression begins.
1933	Hitler becomes German chancellor.
1935	Mussolini invades Ethiopia.
	In Germany, Nuremberg laws deprive Jews of citizenship.
1936	Hitler sends German troops into demilitarized Rhineland.
1936-39	Spanish Civil War.
1937	Japan invades China.
1938	Munich Conference: Britain and France agree to German seizure of part of Czechoslovakia.
1939	Hitler seizes rest of Czechoslovakia. Allies pledge war if Hitler attacks Poland.
	Hitler signs pact with Stalin.
	Germany attacks Poland: World War II begins.

Prepare for the Specific Test

Learn as much as you can about the test you will take. Many instructors give previews of their tests; look at them carefully. If previous tests are available, look them over as well. Try to devise sample questions of your own. If you know, for example, that the test will have identification questions, make a list of items you think might appear. Or if you know that the test will contain long essay questions, try to come up with some of your own. For ideas about possible questions, you can also consult study guides or Web sites that most textbook publishers produce. If the test will contain essay questions and you have previously taken an essay test in the class, examine the way your answers were graded. What were the strengths and weaknesses the instructor noted? Consider how you can build on the strengths and remedy the weaknesses.

Spread your Study over Several Sessions

Research shows that study is more effective when divided into intervals and spread out over time. When preparing for a test, therefore, avoid marathon (and exhausting) all-night sessions. Instead, divide your test preparation into several periods of a couple of hours each.

DURING THE TEST

Plot a Strategy Before You Begin

When you see the test, do not immediately start working. Before answering any questions, go over the whole test. Notice the relative value of each question. Try to estimate how long each answer should take. Then answer the easiest questions first—but watch the clock to ensure that you leave enough time for the questions with the most points. Before answering any question, make sure you understand what it calls for. Finally, be sure to answer all the required questions. Even if you do not know or are not sure of an answer, you may get some credit for trying.

Use the Principles of Good English in Written Answers

In answering questions calling for written answers, follow these principles: Use complete sentences and paragraphs; adopt clear, logical organization; and employ transitions, like *also, in addition,* and *similarly.* Studies have shown a high correlation between the use of such transitions and good grades. Early in every answer, respond to the question, directly and clearly. Make your most important points first. Also, before starting to answer, jot down the points you want to make.

Answer Various Types of Questions Effectively

The most common types of questions on college history tests are identification, matching, short answer, and long essay. Map questions appear frequently, as well. Multiple-choice questions are less common, though not unknown, and students sometimes see true-false items, too. You should know the following facts about these types of questions.

Long-answer essay questions. Most history tests contain such questions. An essay question calls for a genuine essay—written more quickly and without access to written sources—but an essay nevertheless. Thus, your answer should employ complete sentences and effective paragraphs and should be well written in other respects as well. It should also be well organized; grades are often based partly on organization. It should therefore begin with an introduction, containing a clearly stated thesis, which responds directly to the question. The bulk of the answer should then consist of paragraphs developing and supporting this thesis. It should have a conclusion.

Some questions contain questions within the question. These internal questions are intended to guide your answer. Be sure, therefore, to respond specifically to each of them, as well as to the main question. In a world history class, for example, you might encounter a question like this:

> Buddhism and Christianity were both unsuccessful in their original environ-
> ment but unexpectedly successful elsewhere. Discuss the attractions of Bud-
> dhism for China and Japan and its rejection by India. Discuss the success of
> Christianity in the Graeco-Roman world and its rejection by the Jews.

In answering this question, write a general, overarching statement, which will serve as a thesis, about why Buddhism and Christianity were unsuccessful in their original homes and successful elsewhere. You should also discuss all the subjects mentioned in the question: Buddhism in China, Buddhism in Japan, Buddhism in India, Christianity among the Jews, and Christianity in the Graeco-Roman world. In concluding your answer, you could try to show the similarities of Buddhism and Christianity and perhaps the similarities of the environments where they arose.

Make your answer as thorough as you can. When in doubt, say more rather than less. Provide as much specific information from course materials as you can muster. Whenever possible, use information from all materials assigned: lectures, textbooks, other readings. If you can, indicate sources, especially in discussing ideas. Preface a statement with a phrase like, "As Sanchez says . . ."

In asking essay questions, instructors usually seek to see how students think. In answering, therefore, show your thinking processes. Essay questions may ask you to compare and contrast; discuss pros and cons; describe causes or consequences; or evaluate or assess historical developments, events, institutions, or personalities. No matter what the question, all answers should contain a summary statement of your thesis, plus supporting facts and reasoning.

Comparison and contrast questions ask you to describe the similarities and differences of institutions, personalities, or historical developments. In a world history class, for instance, you might be asked to compare European and Japanese feudalism (a feature of both societies). An answer should do more than merely listing differences and similarities: as noted before, it should also argue a thesis, a general point about the similarities and differences. You could organize the body of your answer in two basic ways. In what we might call Plan A, you would discuss the first item in its entirety, then the second item. Following this scheme, a brief outline might look like this:

   I. Introduction
      a. Thesis
  II. European feudalism
 III. Japanese feudalism
  IV. Conclusion

In Plan B, you could compare or contrast each difference or similarity, one at a time:

I. Introduction
   a. Thesis
II. Similarities
   a. Similarity #1
      1. Japan
      2. Europe
   b. Similarity #2
      1. Japan
      2. Europe
III. Differences
   a. Difference #1
      1. Japan
      2. Europe
   b. Difference #2
      1. Japan
      2. Europe
IV. Conclusion

For most people, Plan B works better, allowing, as it does, side-by-side examination of each difference and similarity.

A similar type of question asks for pros and cons; organizing the answer is usually straightforward:

I. Introduction
   a. Thesis
II. Pros
III. Cons
IV. Conclusion

Questions asking for a discussion of causes or consequences also usually dictate a simple organization, such as the following:

I. Introduction
II. Cause #1
III. Cause #2
IV. Cause #3
V. Cause #4
VI. Conclusion

Obviously, the number of causes depends on the question. You can organize answers about consequences the same way.

Questions calling for assessment or evaluation ask for a judgment, your judgment. It is particularly important that you spell this out clearly in a thesis statement early in the paper, preferably in the introduction. In a U.S. history course, for instance, a question might ask, Evaluate Abraham Lincoln's curtailment of civil liberties during the Civil War. In your answer, the thesis statement might read:

> Although some have defended Lincoln's actions, the curtailment of civil liberties during the Civil War was both unnecessary and dangerous.

(You could, of course, take another position.) Whenever possible, a thesis statement should include qualifications (for example, "Although some have defended Lincoln's actions"), showing your understanding that historical questions are complex and can elicit legitimate disagreement among experts.

In organizing answers, writers often state the qualifications first, then discuss their major points. Here is an example:

I. Introduction
  a. Thesis
II. Qualifications
  a. First argument in favor of Lincoln's action
  b. Second argument in favor of Lincoln's action
III. Main Points
  a. Curtailment unnecessary
    1. Fact #1
    2. Fact #2
    3. Fact #3
  b. Dangerous
    1. Fact #1
IV. Conclusion

The number of points in each section will vary, of course, depending on your answer.

Identification. These questions are also common. Such questions frequently present students with a list of terms—names, events, concepts—from which they are supposed to choose a certain number: ten out of fifteen, for example, or five out of eight. If given such a choice, choose the ones you know best. Do not try to answer them all. In most cases you get credit for only a certain number; if you answer more, you just waste valuable time.

Sometimes instructors tell you what answers should include. Follow such instructions. Otherwise, say as much as you can about each item in the time available. If possible, indicate the *who, what, when, where,* and *why* of each item (some instructors tell you this; many merely expect it). Indicate each item's *historical significance*—almost all instructors expect students to do this. Write clearly, in complete sentences.

Matching, multiple-choice, true-false. Matching questions are also common, usually consisting of two columns of items. These questions seldom require complex test-taking techniques; simply begin by matching the items you are sure of, leaving any questionable ones until later.

With multiple-choice questions, look at the instructions carefully. Do they ask for the right answer or the best answer? Best-answer questions are trickier; the best answer might be partly wrong. People who write multiple-choice tests have to come up with three or four wrong answers for every right one. Correct answers are usually carefully qualified, while incorrect ones may not be. Too simple answers are often wrong. Knowing this, however, a test writer will sometimes make the correct answer the simplest. You should also watch any qualifiers in the answers; they can easily make a plausible-sounding answer wrong. Also, answers with the most moderate qualifiers are likely to be correct. Finally, your first impression is most likely to be correct. Do not change your answers unless you are absolutely certain. True-false questions are even rarer (fortunately, in the opinion of many students, who find them tricky). In such questions, any false detail makes the whole answer false.

QUICK REVIEW: TESTS

- **Studying:** Concentrate on the important points, put material from different sources together, organize the material for yourself as you study, prepare for the specific test, and spread your study over several sessions.

- **Taking tests:** Plot a strategy before you begin, use the principles of good English in written answers, and employ the right strategy for each question.

CHAPTER 7

USING THE INTERNET TO STUDY HISTORY

AT A GLANCE

- Know how your history classes use the Internet.
- Make the most effective use of e-mail in a course.
- Evaluate Web sites for accuracy and usefulness.
- Find history material on the Web—using search engines, databases, online reference materials, library catalogs, publishers' Web sites, and other important history Web locations.

As in many other fields, the Internet is dramatically changing the study of history. The Internet, of course, consists of millions of computers around the world linked to each other so that they can share data. The World Wide Web ("the Web") enables historians and history students to read articles, find documents, see pictures, listen to music, and view movies right on their computer screens. Another aspect of this network, e-mail, has become an important tool for scholars, who can now exchange information and ideas with others no matter where they are. It also allows students and professors to communicate in ways they never could before. In most history courses, using the Internet is helpful; in an increasing number it is a necessity. This chapter provides information about how history students can use the Internet effectively.

KNOW HOW YOUR HISTORY COURSE USES THE INTERNET

History classes vary in the extent to which they use the Internet. Many instructors put their syllabi on the Internet; others maintain class Web sites of differing degrees of complexity, which may contain the syllabus, the schedule, study guides, lecture outlines, instructor's notes, and writing assignments. In any class, be sure to familiarize yourself with whatever material your instructor has provided. Some of it may be essential; all of it will give you insight into your instructor's approach to the class, which may prove invaluable.

Another use of the Internet is discussion, which can occur in various formats. One is the electronic bulletin board, a site on the World Wide Web where messages are posted. A related form is the newsgroup, where readers can read messages and respond with comments of their own, typically by filling in a form on the Web site. The comments are then displayed on the site, usually in the order in which they are received. An instructor may also use a "listserve," a list containing the e-mail addresses of all participants, allowing anyone in the class to send a message to a single address and reach the whole group. Another device is the chat room—a listserve in which participants are at their computers at the same time to read and answer messages as they come in.

Instructors may also use class-management software programs, like ANGEL and Blackboard, to coordinate Internet class activities. These programs can give students access to syllabi, announcements, schedules, assignments, lecture notes, articles, maps, and other images. They also have features allowing students to take quizzes and tests and receive scores and other kinds of responses online. In addition, these programs have online grade books, which enable the instructor to post scores for students to see over the Internet. If your instructor uses such a program, be sure to master it.

USE E-MAIL EFFECTIVELY

In many classes instructors expect students to communicate with them electronically, and some actually prefer e-mail to telephone calls. Professors increasingly maintain "virtual office hours": set times in which they read and respond to e-mail as they receive it. Many also accept or welcome written assignments turned in by e-mail; some even require this method of submission.

In a history class it is important to use e-mail effectively, especially when writing to your instructor. Be sure to indicate clearly who you are and what you are discussing. Most teachers have several classes, sometimes several different sections of the same class—and many students. They may not instantly recognize your name, especially at the beginning of a term, and particularly if you have not attended class yet. Many instructors, for instance, have received messages like this, sent to the fictitious Professor Elizabeth Steele at Any University:

To: esteele@anyuniv.edu

From: goodtimeboy-sos@yahoo.com

About: class

ive just enrolled in class but i haven't heard anything from u. are u
my teacher send me what i need right away sean

This message will probably make a bad impression. Not only does it lack punctuation and capitalization, but it may take the fictitious Professor Steele a while
to figure out who "Sean" is and what class he is in (if he is actually in one of
hers). When you write, give your instructor as much information as possible, in
the "subject" box as well as in your message. "Sean," for example, might write:

To: Professor Elizabeth Steele esteele@anyuniv.edu

Subject: Late enrollment in World History, MWF 11:00

Dear Professor Steele,
I have just enrolled in your class, World History (MWF 11:00-12:00).
I apologize for my late enrollment. If possible, could you please
e-mail me a copy of your syllabus and any other introductory
material available? If e-mail is not convenient, I would be happy
to go by your office during your office hours or pick up the material
in class.

Sean Richards

The second message illustrates the virtues of e-mail etiquette. First, in the
"subject" line, Sean indicates what class he is in and exactly what the message is about. Second, he employs Standard English, which you should use
unless you receive instructions to the contrary. This means normal capitalization, college-level grammar, and complete sentences and paragraphs. Third,
although many people are accustomed to extreme informality on the Internet,
it is a good idea to address your instructor with a certain amount of defer-
ence, using a title she or he prefers. Many want to be called "Professor," "Dr.,"
"Mr.," or "Ms."; their syllabi may give you a clue. But if you do not know the
preference, "Professor" is always safe. Do not use first names unless you have
received permission to do so. You should also, of course, avoid an accusatory
approach, such as "I've written you three times and haven't heard anything

from you yet." Moreover, since most faculty members are busy, some do not read or respond to e-mail every day. When you write, therefore, do not automatically expect an immediate response—and plan accordingly.

Show courtesy to your fellow students, as well, either when writing to them individually or in e-mail discussions. Avoid "flaming" (insulting language), and remember that e-mail often sounds more aggressive than the writer intends. Read your messages before you send them, and tone down any harsh-sounding language.

Instructors often give specific instructions about the format of assignments submitted by e-mail. They may require students to use college or university e-mail accounts or to submit assignments in either the body of an e-mail message or as an attachment, using certain programs, such as Microsoft Word. You should follow these instructions punctiliously.

THE WORLD WIDE WEB

The Web, as it is known, provides a powerful tool for gathering information on almost any subject, including history. Here are the basics: Each Web site contains one or more pages. Each page has an address, or URL (uniform resource locator), consisting of the characters *http://* followed by other characters that identify the file. It often includes an identifier that tells what kind of site it is, such as *com* for commercial sites, *org* for organizations, or *edu* for colleges and universities. Usually, you do not have to type *http://*—just the rest of the ULR. You can also get to Web pages through a hyperlink: characters that are encoded so that clicking your mouse button while the cursor is on them will take you automatically to the Web site. To look at Web pages, you need a software program called a Web browser. The most popular is Microsoft Internet Explorer, but there are others as well. Most computers come with browsers, but you can download them, often at no cost, especially if you are a student, simply by going to the browser's Web site.

The Web is always in flux: Sites appear, disappear, and change. In this dynamic, freewheeling virtual atmosphere, you must safeguard any material you get. Whenever you find a page you think might be useful, download or print it, preferably both. The page could change or even disappear by the next time you try to use it again. (You can, however, often find these pages by using the Wayback Machine: http://www.archive.org/web/web.php.)

Evaluating Web Sites

The Web consists of a vast number of sites around the word, millions, actually, maintained by every conceivable type of person or organization, from grade school students to terrorist organizations. The Web allows you to read the catalogs of libraries and archives around the world, get primary source documents and statistics, and read articles, even books, on your computer. It also presents potential pitfalls. Almost anyone can create a Web site and put anything on it, from scientific papers to pornography. It is essential, therefore, to evaluate every Web site you intend to use. In doing so, you may find the following checklist helpful:

- **Who is the author?** Failure to indicate the author's identity may be a danger sign. At the very least, it makes the site's reliability hard to assess. If the author is not immediately identifiable, you can sometimes find that information by going to the Web site's home page. If you know who the author is, ask yourself what his or her credentials are. Are they academic? Is the author associated with a college or university? If so, is it reputable? What is the author's connection to the institution? Is he or she a professor, or a student? On nonacademic Web sites, does the author claim to be a journalist? If so, is he or she affiliated with a reputable publication?

- **Who maintains the site, and what are its purposes?** Is it a government institution, political organization, a for-profit company? If the site does not indicate who maintains it, you may have a hard time determining its credibility. If you can identify the sponsoring organization, you should try to determine what its purpose is.

  If a business maintains the site, it will undoubtedly seek to create a favorable public image and therefore will present information that portrays itself in the best light possible. That does not mean it is not telling the truth. Most large corporations check their facts carefully. But the information will be designed to make the company look as good as possible.

  Is the Web site affiliated with an academic institution? College and university Web sites can have a wide variety of content. Material posted by a professor will represent that professor's viewpoint. Most professors carefully check their facts, but since scholarship is a process of debate, not all experts may agree with that professor. More mundane information at college and university Web sites, like course descriptions, calendars, and other institutional materials, will be as accurate as the institutions can make them. Items posted by students are only as reliable as the students posting them; the fact that they are on a college or university Web site does not in itself make them accurate.

  Nonprofit organizations sponsor Web sites. These organizations range from large national institutions, like the Ford Foundation, to neighborhood groups. Most use their Web sites to promote their own goals, as well as provide information. In evaluating them, consider the causes they are promoting. Political organizations also maintain Web sites. Organizations ranging from the National Rifle Association to the Sierra Club seek to advance their causes on their Web sites. So do ideologically oriented think tanks, like the liberal Brookings Institution and the conservative American Enterprise Institute and Heritage Foundation. Political parties, like the Republicans and the Democrats, also maintain active Web sites, which they use to attack opponents and promote their own members. You should not be afraid of using such Web sites. Authors with strong viewpoints do not necessarily misstate the facts. But an intelligent user of the Internet should be aware of a site or an author's political orientation.

At the same time, it is important to emphasize that vigorous advocacy of a position does not mean the site (or book or article) is either untrustworthy or wrong. Many students are so afraid of "bias" that they distrust anything other than strict neutrality. In journalism, history, and many other fields, however, books and articles often advance a thesis, and authors frequently write to promote their own ideas. Students should expect this and learn to identify the points being argued; but they should not assume that such writing is unreliable.

• **How convincing are the contents?** Look at the contents themselves. Do they provide evidence for their assertions? Do they cite sources? The need for evidence varies, of course, with the type of information you are examining. You do not have to worry much about visiting hours at Thomas Jefferson's home, Monticello, but you should look critically at an article about Franklin Roosevelt's mistakes in dealing with the Great Depression.

Whenever possible, compare the information on the Web site with other sources you know to be reliable. The first step might be to compare it to your textbook, which was written and carefully checked by experts. Also, you can compare a Web site to others maintained elsewhere by reputable sources, like encyclopedias or U.S. government Web sites.

FINDING MATERIAL ON THE INTERNET

For history students, useful tools for finding information are search engines, databases (usually available through your college or university library), general reference sites (like dictionaries), and library catalogs, almost all of which are now online. Students studying textbooks can usually also use Web sites maintained by their books' publishers to help them in their study.

Search Engines

The basic tool for finding Web sites is the search engine. Currently, the dominant search engine is Google (www.google.com); according to a recent survey, almost half of all searches used it. The ubiquity of Google has even produced a new verb—"to google"—meaning to use Google to find material on the Web. Unlike some older search engines, Google uses software rather than human editors to explore the Web, collect information, and classify sites.

Google also operates a variation of its main search engine, Google Scholar (http://scholar.google.com), which is designed specifically for academic purposes. In its Beta (developmental) version, it searches the Web for books, articles, dissertations, theses, abstracts, technical reports, and Web sites. When Google Scholar displays an entry for a book, it also shows hyperlinks that may lead to libraries that have the book, sites that offer the book for sale, the online text of the book, or articles and books that cite it, which the user can often read online. The material available varies, of course. Advanced Scholar Search, a feature available from the main Google Scholar page, also allows further refinements of searches.

Other popular search engines are Yahoo (www.yahoo.com), MSN (www.msn.com), and Ask.com (www.ask.com). In general, these engines are better adapted for commercial than academic searches. Since the Internet is always changing, search engines can change their names, be redesigned, and lose or gain dominance. It is useful from time to time, therefore, to try different search engines. To keep up to date on search engines, you can go to Web sites that cover them, like Search Engine Watch (www.searchenginewatch.com).

In general, when using a search engine, the more specific your search, the better. If, for example, you were looking for information on the American women's rights leader Susan B. Anthony, you could type in just "Anthony." A Google search using just this name might produce Web sites on various Anthony's restaurants, the actor Anthony Hopkins, the religious figure St. Anthony, and various other Anthonys. If, however, you typed in "Susan B Anthony," all of the first ten Web sites would probably deal with the feminist leader rather than other, irrelevant, people.

It is sometimes useful to know search engine math. Many search engines use mathematical signs to refine searches. The plus sign (+) lets you make sure that the Web site you are seeking contains all the words in your search. For example, to find Web sites that contain the words *slave* and *women*, you would type

+ slave + women

The minus sign (–), on the other hand, lets the user exclude words, that is, avoid Web sites that contain certain words. Perhaps, for example, you were looking for information on the history of the diesel engine and your search produced a lot of Web sites about the actor Vin Diesel. Using the minus sign, you could avoid the Vin Diesel Web sites by typing

diesel – Vin

In using the minus sign, make sure to leave a space between the preceding word and the minus. Without the space, some search engines treat the minus like a comma and give you only sites containing both words.

Sometimes you will want to find only Web pages that contain certain phrases, or combinations of words. In that case, use quotation marks. You might, for example, want to search for Web sites about Otto von Bismarck, the nineteenth-century German chancellor, while avoiding sites about Bismarck, North Dakota, and the Bismarck pastry. In that case, type "Otto von Bismarck"; doing so will produce only sites with those three words in that order. Using quotation marks, however, presents certain pitfalls. In your Otto von Bismarck search, you probably also want sites with the words *Bismarck,*

Otto von and even *Bismarck, Otto.* "Otto von Bismarck" would not produce those. It might be wiser in that case to use a plus-sign search for +Otto+Bismarck. Such a search would also turn up Web sites titled "Prince Otto von Bismarck" and "Fuerst ['Prince' in German] von Bismarck."

You can also combine search math signs. You might, for example, want sites about John F. Kennedy as a young man. You are not sure that the phrase "President John Kennedy" will get sites about his youth, and you want to avoid those about his son, John F. Kennedy, Jr. In that case, type

+ Kennedy + John + young – Jr

In addition to using search engine math, many search engines also have their own advanced search features. These vary from engine to engine; so it is best to read the description of these features provided by the search engine, usually through a hyperlink at the top of the main page.

Databases

Databases—usually available through libraries—are valuable sources of information. Some are on CDs, which students can sometimes check out, but, increasingly, they are accessible over the Internet. Libraries may provide access to either the general public or to only college or university students and faculty members. Since the number of databases continues to grow, it is useful to check with a librarian when you are looking for information. At present, here are some of the most important:

Expanded Academic ASAP contains many history periodicals (with the full text of their contents), among them the *Journal of American History*, the *Journal of Family History*, the *Journal of the History of Ideas*, and the *Journal of the History of Philosophy*. As of this printing, it did not include the *American Historical Review*, the official publication of the American Historical Association, but it may add this and other journals as time goes on. As with all electronic media, changes can take place quickly.

JSTOR is a database containing major historical journals published in the United States and some published in Great Britain. Libraries can subscribe to different groups of publications in the database; check your library's current holdings at the time you use it. Like other databases, JSTOR has a search feature.

PROQUEST is a database of newspapers. The holdings available depend on the library's subscription. The most common is probably the historical *New York Times*, which contains past editions of this newspaper.

Historical Abstracts contains abstracts (summaries) of journal articles covering all countries except the United States and Canada (which are found in *America: History and Life*, described below). Most abstracts range from 75 to 120 words; those the editors deem less significant receive one- or two-sentence summaries rather than full reviews. This database also contains citations to important books reviewed in journals and some dissertations. Students doing research in an area of history covered by this database will find it useful in locating articles and getting a sense of what historians are doing in the field. Users can search by key word, subject, title, and author; they can also use other, more sophisticated search techniques. Large research university libraries usually have this database and provide access to their students; smaller libraries sometimes do not.

America: History and Life is the companion database to *Historical Abstracts* and covers the United States and Canada. It provides material in the same format and is similarly useful for research in American and Canadian history.

Arts and Humanities Search provides an index to over 1300 journals in the arts and humanities from around world, including, but not restricted to, history. Students doing research might want to consult it to augment what they have found in history indexes. In addition to its arts and humanities journal references, it also contains selected citations from social science and science publications that the editors think relevant to arts and humanities researchers. It covers periodicals going back to 1984 and is updated weekly.

The *Humanities Index* is an index to articles in the humanities, including history, and is an important resource for history research. In many libraries the database has replaced the printed version of this index. The database indexes articles back to 1974. For earlier articles, use the *Humanities & Social Sciences Index Retrospective*.

Social Sciences Index is a companion to the *Humanities Index*. It provides citations to articles in the social sciences, some of which may be useful for historical research. It also appears in printed form, but the database usually provides easier searching. Like the *Humanities Index*, it goes back to 1974. For older articles, see the *Humanities & Social Sciences Index Retrospective*, mentioned above.

As previously noted, for pre-1974 articles the *Humanities & Social Sciences Index Retrospective* takes the place of the *Humanities Index* and *Social Science Index* (published by the same company, H.W. Wilson). This database provides citations going back to 1907.

Social Scisearch is an index to the social sciences. Since some articles of interest to historians may be classified as social science, a thorough search might include this database.

Dissertation Abstracts. Students doing advanced research may want to find out if dissertations (written by graduate students working toward doctorates) contain information useful in their research. This database enables you to find and download dissertations. Most universities granting doctoral degrees subscribe to this database, although smaller college libraries may not.

RLG Union Catalog. Formerly known as RLIN, this database can be useful for advanced students. It is available to students and faculty members at most research universities and many other colleges and universities. As a union catalog, it indexes the holdings of many libraries and other research institutions around the world, which include books, periodicals, maps, manuscripts, recordings, and other types of materials.

Research Navigator (www.researchnavigator.com). Maintained by the publisher Prentice Hall for students who have purchased its textbooks, this site currently contains four databases for research. For history, the most important of these is the "EBSCO/ContentSelect" Academic Journal and Abstract Database, which allows searches of numerous articles in popular and scholarly periodicals. Full-text content is available for many of them. The site also gives free access to the *New York Times* archive for the past year plus the *Financial Times* one-year archive and that publication's five-year collection of corporate financial reports. The site includes a "Link Library," a collection of Web sites selected by the editors for usefulness and reliability. Research Navigator also has information on conducting research and writing research papers, with guidance on citing sources and avoiding plagiarism, plus a reference guide to grammar. At present, a user name and password are required for access.

Online Reference Materials

The Internet also provides access to many other reference materials. Dictionaries and thesauruses, for example, are available on a number of Web sites. Merriam-Webster (http://www.merriam-webster.com/) provides an online dictionary; Bartelby.com (http://www.bartleby.com/61/) contains the *American Heritage Dictionary*. Also available online is the *Oxford English Dictionary*, which describes the history of every English word. Although a subscription is required for access, many college and university libraries make it available to students. Other online dictionaries are at YourDictionary.com (http://www .yourdictionary.com/) and Dictionary.com (http://dictionary.reference.com/). If you need a foreign language dictionary, you can also find it on the Web. Just go to a search engine, like Google, and type "German dictionary" or "Spanish dictionary"; you will get pages of links.

Encyclopedias are also available online. Currently, the *Encyclopedia Britannica* requires a subscription for online access, but many libraries make it available to their students and faculty. The *Columbia Encyclopedia* is available free at a number of sites, including Bartelby.com/, Information Please (http:// www.infoplease.com/), and High Beam Research (http://www.highbeam .com/ref/). Microsoft, of course, provides the Encarta encyclopedia (http:// encarta.msn.com/). Since the Web is constantly changing, when you want an encyclopedia, the best thing is simply to do a search.

Bartleby also makes several important books of quotations available, including *Bartlett's Familiar Quotations*. If you have a question about correct English usage, you can check with Bartleby or Dictionary.com, which, in addition to online dictionaries, provides access to several guides to grammar, usage, and style. High Beam Research currently allows users to search several kinds of reference works, including encyclopedias, dictionaries, thesauruses, and, as noted above, the *Columbia Encyclopedia*. Information Please provides almanacs, an atlas, a dictionary, and a thesaurus, as well as the *Columbia Encyclopedia*. Some major guides to history are also now on the Web, including *The Reader's Companion to American History*, which users can search at Answers.com (http://www.answers.com/library/American%20History). This site also contains a dictionary, a thesaurus, and the ubiquitous *Columbia Encyclopedia*.

Library Catalogs

For history students, one of the most useful tools is a library catalog, most of which are now online. These probably include those of your own college or university libraries, as well as most other institutions in the United States and Canada. Using the Internet, you can quickly find what books and periodicals a library has. After your own library's catalog, perhaps the most important is that of the Library of Congress (http://www.loc.gov/), which lists all books ever published in the United States, and many others as well.

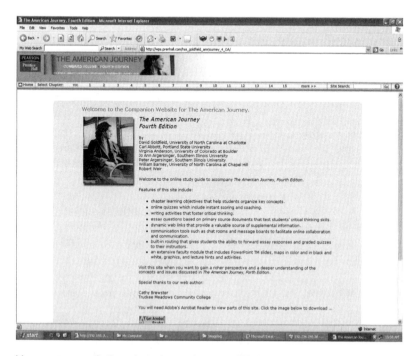

Home page of the *American Journey* Web site, http://wps.prenhall.com/has_goldfield_amrjourney_4_OA.

Publishers' Web Sites

Many textbook publishers provide Web sites containing features to help students study the books they publish. These may include chapter and section summaries, glossaries or lists of key words, study questions, maps, pictures, documents, map exercises, practice questions, and links to Web sites with further information about topics covered in a chapter. These sites may also provide space for your instructor to post the course syllabus and other material, as well as electronic bulletin boards and access to threaded discussions. For example, the Web site for the U.S. history textbook *The American Journey* by David Goldfield et al. (www.prenhall.com/goldfield) contains a link to material for each chapter. This material includes a chapter summary, learning objectives, and practice tests. For each section within a chapter, students can also find summaries and sample questions, materials for thinking about the section, images, documents, and map-labeling exercises. The site also contains links to sites containing related material.

Useful History Web Sites

A comprehensive guide to history is the WWW VL (World Wide Web Virtual Library) History Central Catalogue (http://vlib.iue.it/history/index.html). This has links to a vast number of sites useful in the study of history. Many of the links are organized by region and country. This site also contains links to more general Web sites, including aids to finding material, maps, general reference works, publications, scholarships, and even information about careers in history.

Another important history Web site is maintained by the Library of Congress (www.loc.gov). It contains the American Memory collection, which consists of written documents, images, and sounds, available over the Internet. These, by the way, are not restricted to history but include a wide variety of disciplines, from agriculture to technology, many of which may prove useful to history students. The Library of Congress site also allows online access to research guides, general reference works, and information about doing research.

Other Web sites are also important sources for primary source documents. In European history, an invaluable site is "EuroDocs: Online Sources for European History" (http://eudocs.lib.byu.edu/index.php/Main_Page), maintained by Brigham Young University. Researchers working in medieval European history will find "The Labyrinth: Resources for Medieval Study" (http://labyrinth.georgetown.edu/) useful.

Documents in American history are available from the Historical Text Archive (http://historicaltextarchive.com/), maintained by Donald J. Mabry. It contains several hundred documents, articles, and books, which can be read online. The site organizes the material by subject and region. It includes short biographical articles, unsigned articles on historical periods or movements, and documents.

The Avalon Project at Yale University Law School provides online access to important American political documents (http://www.yale.edu/lawweb/avalon/avalon.htm). Its pre-eighteenth-century collection includes legal documents ranging from the Code of Hammurabi and the Athenian Constitution to the charters of the American colonies. Documents from the eighteenth century to the present include treaties, legislation, important speeches, and court cases. Similar documents are available at a site maintained by the University of Groningen in the Netherlands (http://odur.let.rug.nl/~usa/D/). In addition, the "Chronology of U.S. Historical Documents," maintained by the University of Oklahoma College of Law (http://www.law.ou.edu/hist/), also provides online access to U.S. political and diplomatic documents. At the time of this writing, it contained the inaugural addresses of the American presidents. The National Archives Web site (http://www.archives.gov/index.html) is also an important source of documents of this sort, along with other interesting digital material.

The "Digital History" Web site at the University of Houston (http://www.digitalhistory.uh.edu/hyperhistorian.cfm) has several collections of documents available online. It includes a section called the "Boisterous Sea of Liberty," which contains documents written by members of the Revolutionary War generation. Another section is "Historic Newspapers." The "Landmark Documents" section contains mostly political documents in American history, ranging from the Magna Carta to Kenneth Starr's report on President Bill Clinton. Other sections contain documents relating to the history of American ethnic groups. The History Matters Web site (http://historymatters.gmu.edu/) is designed for history teachers and students, especially teachers. However, it has a document collection that concentrates on the experience of ordinary rather than famous persons.

Other sites offer documents in specialized areas of American history. The "Making of America" project at the University of Michigan (http://www.hti.umich.edu/m/moagrp/) provides social history documents from the antebellum (pre–Civil War) period through Reconstruction. "Documenting the American South" from the University of North Carolina (http://www.hti.umich.edu/m/moagrp/) contains a wide range of documents in Southern history, with emphasis, understandably enough, on North Carolina. The collections include "First-Person Narratives of the American South"; the "Library of Southern Literature" (which contains many historic travel books about the South); "North American Slave Narratives"; "The Southern Homefront, 1861–1865"; "The Church in the Southern Black Community," "The North Carolina Experience, Beginnings to 1940"; and "North Carolinians and the Great War." The Chicago Historical Society has a collection of documents relating to the Haymarket Affair—a controversial 1886 bombing and battle between the police and anarchist protesters. This is located at the Haymarket Affair Digital Library (http://www.chicagohs.org/hadc/index.html).

Students interested in the Salem witch trials will find the complete court documents from this case at http://etext.virginia.edu/salem/witchcraft. Many books are now available online as well. A leading site is Project Gutenberg (http://www.gutenberg.net/), which was a pioneer in putting books on the Internet. It contains thousands of books in many languages, which you can read over the Internet or print out if you are willing to use a lot of paper. Most of these books are old and out of copyright, as are those on other Web sites offering digitized books. You are not likely, therefore, to find the most recent best seller, but you may find valuable things. Other sites providing books online include the Online Books Page (http://digital.library .upenn.edu/books/), which has more than twenty thousand books, and the University of Virginia Electronic Text Center (http://etext.lib.virginia.edu/). In addition, Bartleby.com (www.bartleby.com) provides selected works of fiction and nonfiction, most of which are classics or standard works.

A FINAL NOTE

Anyone using the Internet must remember that it is always changing. Many of the Web pages and materials described here did not exist a few years ago, and the resources available a couple of years from now may be vastly different— probably much more extensive. So keep in mind that any existing Web page may disappear and that many new ones will surely come onto the scene, giving you far more information, documents, and images than are currently available. Current Web sites also frequently change their purposes, function, design, and even their addresses (URLs). As you use the Internet to study history, therefore, do not be satisfied with what you know; always look for new material and new tools to find and use.

QUICK REVIEW

- **To make the best use of the Internet,** learn how your history class uses the Internet; follow the suggestion in this chapter for using e-mail; evaluate Web sites for accuracy and usefulness (see checklist); and use search engines, databases, online reference material, library catalogs, and other important history Web sites to find material for classes.

CHAPTER 8

HOW TO WRITE SHORT PAPERS FOR HISTORY CLASSES

AT A GLANCE

To Write Efficiently
- Make notes.
- Draft a tentative thesis.
- Arrange your notes in order.
- Develop an introduction.
- Write a first draft.
- Revise.
- Produce a final draft.

To Write a Short Essay
- Adopt a thesis.
- List the arguments for and against it.
- Follow the organization recommended.
- Follow the efficient writing process of making notes, arranging them in order, making an outline, writing a first draft, revising, writing a final draft, and proofreading.

To Write Comparisons
- Make a list of similarities and differences.
- Draft a thesis.
- Convert the similarities and differences into notes and follow the rest of the writing process.

(continued)

To Write a Book Review
- Read the book, making notes on the contents, interpretation, main points, persuasiveness, organization and style, and similarities to or differences from similar books.
- Organize your notes, write your first draft, revise, and prepare a final draft.

Most history courses require writing. This chapter tells you how to write the most common types of short assignments, including short essays, comparisons, and book reviews. For information on writing a full-length research paper, see Chapter 9.

WRITING EFFICIENTLY

When you write, you need an efficient procedure. While experienced writers use different techniques, here is a tried-and-tested process that will enable you to move effectively from assignment to finished piece of writing. You can use it for any kind of writing project, from a book review or short analytical essay to a long research paper.

Making Notes

Once you have decided on a subject, the first step is to make notes. To do so, put all of your thoughts into notes. If you do not seem to have many thoughts on the subject, brainstorm—write down everything you can think of, no matter how far-fetched it may seem at the time—and put it into notes. Later on, you can discard points that no longer seem worthwhile. At this stage it is often helpful to review your lecture notes and those you have made about your textbook; they may give you ideas.

Your notes should be in a form that lets you easily rearrange them. You can write them by hand, putting them on pieces of paper or cards of any size, or you can type them on your computer. If you write them by hand, use a pen; notes written in pencil can smear, making them illegible. For most people in this computer-literate age, using a computer is the most efficient method, since you can probably type faster than you can write by hand. Perhaps even more important, computers allow easy cutting, pasting, and rearranging. When making notes, be sure to indicate on each note the source of all facts or ideas. Include the author, title, place of publication, publisher, year of publication, page numbers, and any other information needed for a foot- or endnote (for more information, see Chapter 10, "Citing Your Sources"). This will be essential if you need citations; and even if they are unnecessary, having this information recorded can be helpful later on.

At various stages in the writing process, you may want to engage in "free writing." This is a process in which you simply sit down and write without planning and usually without hesitating. Free writing can help you develop thoughts, organize your thinking, or come up with wording you may want to use in the future. You may choose to use pieces of free writing or discard them altogether.

Drafting a Tentative Thesis

Second, draft a tentative thesis, a statement of the main point you want to make. Many instructors explicitly require such a statement. Even if it is not required, include one anyway; it will help you keep your writing focused.

A thesis must be debatable. It should not be something obvious or something that everyone already agrees with, like "The U.S. Civil War began in 1861." That is simply a statement of fact. Rather, it should be a point about which reasonable people can disagree. Some students are surprised at being expected to make an argument in a history paper, since much historical writing looks like description or narration. But most is actually persuasive writing. Generally, historians do not describe events merely for their own sake, but to persuade readers (who are often other historians).

If you really wanted to make the Civil War statement above into a usable thesis, you might argue that the war could not have begun earlier, in 1851, for example, or 1841. Your thesis could then say "The Civil War could not have begun before 1861 because the necessary conditions had not been fulfilled." In that case, you would have a legitimate—a debatable—thesis.

How do you come up with a thesis? Sometimes, of course, you may already know what you want to say, but if not, here is a procedure you may find helpful:

Look over the material you are supposed to write about. Jot down any possible points you think of. These do not have to be profound, and you do not even have to use them in your final draft. But writing them down will help you get started. Then consider what you already know about the subject. Jot down those ideas as well. You might also reread your lecture notes and the notes or markings in your text and other books. Write down anything that occurs to you. Then go through what you have and look for every possible thesis.

What if you fail to find one you like? In that case, choose the most promising. Then think of ways to modify it, ideally, to make it more complex. It does not have to be perfect; you can continue to change it whenever you want. But at least by this point, you will have something you can use.

Organizing your Ideas

Once you have come up with a tentative thesis, the next step is to arrange your notes in order. If you have written them by hand, you can spread them out on a table or even the floor—a time-honored ritual of student life. If you wrote them on a computer (highly recommended), you can rearrange them there. When you do, it is a good idea to open a new file, copy the notes into it, and keep the old file intact rather than rearranging the notes in the old one. In that way, if you accidentally change or delete something from your notes or ever wonder about a note's accuracy, you can refer to the originals.

Once you have arranged the notes, look them over. You might even want to print them out so you can see them on paper. As you look at them, you may want to rearrange them again. Do not be afraid to change, add, or delete things until you feel comfortable with what you are going to say and how you are going to say it (or until you run out of time).

As you arrange your notes, create an outline. This does not have to be formal, with Roman numerals and letters, or anything like that. It should just be a list of the subjects you want to discuss or points you want to make in the order in which you want to make them. When you finish arranging your notes, revise the outline to reflect the final organization.

Writing a First Draft

Your next job is writing the first draft. As you do, try to write continuously, as if you are telling someone a story. Just look at your notes and write; when you finish with one note, go on to the next one. If you are writing on a computer, you can use your notes or outline in several ways. First, you can copy and paste your outline into the new file in which you intend to write the first draft. You can then fill in the outline using paragraphs and sentences. You may decide to retain parts of the outline as headings and subheadings, or you may delete them. Second, you can copy and paste all of your notes (arranged in order) into the new, first-draft file. You can then write, using the notes: rewording them, adding introductions, discussions, and summaries to them and writing transitions to the material covered in the next note. Third, you can keep the notes, the outline, or both in another file and refer to them as you write. You can do this by having two windows open—one with the notes or outline and the other with the first draft. Or you can toggle back and forth between files.

At this stage it makes no difference whether your writing seems good or not. The important thing is to get the whole paper written down.

At some point, write an introduction. Some people like to do this before writing the rest of the paper. Others write the other parts first and work on the introduction afterward. You can decide which method works best for you. An introduction does not have to be perfect at first. The important thing is to get it written down. Later, you may have better ideas for it, perhaps even a clearer picture of what you want to say in the paper as a whole. In any case, you can rework it, along with the rest of the paper.

Regardless of when you write the introduction, it will usually do the following: indicate the subject, suggest why the subject is important, and state your thesis, or point of view. Which of these parts should come first? There is no hard-and-fast rule, but you will generally find the following order most effective: (1) importance of subject, (2) indication of the subject, and (3) thesis statement.

Let's take a typical assignment, this one on Reconstruction (which followed the American Civil War). During this period, a split developed among Northern reformers. One group maintained that guaranteeing African-American men the vote was more urgent than obtaining it simultaneously for women. Developing sufficient political support for women's suffrage, they argued, would derail the attainment of African-American voting rights. Others insisted that African-Americans and women should receive the vote at the same time. Those advocating the first position won: The Constitution guaranteed black male suffrage in the 1860s, and women had to wait until 1919 for a Constitutional guarantee. With this in mind, suppose the assignment were as follows: "Discuss the relationship of Reconstruction policies and the women's movement."[1] In writing the introduction, you could begin by commenting on the significance of your subject; you could then identify it, and, finally, you could state your thesis—as in this example:

> The Reconstruction period proved a watershed for the women's movement. Proponents of African-American suffrage, believing that they were forced to choose between voting rights for black men and the advancement of suffrage for women, chose black male suffrage. The results for women were tragic. The abandonment of female suffrage by former Radicals led women's voting rights proponents, such as Elizabeth Cady Stanton, to descend into racism; and the Constitutional right to vote for women was postponed until 1919. Moreover, the choice was unnecessary: Had Radicals maintained an equal commitment to both goals, both could have been achieved.

Notice the order. First, a general statement suggests the importance of the subject ("The Reconstruction period proved a watershed for the women's movement."). Then the author identifies the subject (the Radicals' abandonment of women's suffrage in favor of the vote for black men). In between, connecting sentences link these two elements together. Finally, we have graceful passage to the thesis ("Had Radicals maintained an equal commitment to both goals, both could have been achieved").

Revising

Once you have finished the rough draft, set it aside for a while—a few hours, or a couple of days, if you have the time. Then go back and edit it. Change paragraphs, sentences, and words. Correct grammatical errors. Read the paper aloud to yourself or, even better, to a friend. Reading it aloud will help you find mistakes and awkward places. If you have time, go through the same editing process on a second draft. Most professional writers write many more than two.

Writing a Final Draft

When you have finished your revisions, incorporate them into a final draft. If possible, also set this aside for a while, just as you did with the earlier drafts. Be sure to proofread it carefully. Use your computer's spell checker, but do not rely on it. Check anything you have doubts about by looking it up in a dictionary or a writing handbook.

WRITING SHORT ESSAYS

History instructors often assign short essays with a variety of appellations: critical essays, discussion papers, and analytical essays. In writing an assignment of this kind, follow the techniques of efficient writing described earlier in this chapter. First, put your thoughts into notes. Once you have made your notes, draft a tentative thesis. Next, list all the arguments in favor of your thesis. Then list all those against it. At this point, organize your notes in the order in which they will appear in the paper. The notes should contain everything you intend to say in your essay. If you think of other points as you arrange the notes, make more notes.

As you arrange your notes, create an outline. Most short essays are organized in the following way:

- Introduction, including statement of thesis
- Rebuttal of arguments that could be made against the thesis
- Discussion of arguments in favor of the thesis
- Conclusion

This organization shows the rebuttal of arguments against the thesis preceding the discussion of those in its favor. Recently, some experts have argued for the opposite arrangement. They advocate following the "law of primacy," which says, "People tend to remember best what they read first." Following this rule would mean putting the arguments in favor of your thesis first, in fact, putting your strongest argument at the very beginning of that section. From Aristotle on, however, rhetoricians have contended that you should discuss and refute the opposing arguments first, then make the arguments in favor of your position in detail, giving the evidence and reasoning to support each argument. If you follow this rule, you will be using a time-tested technique. In addition, this traditional organization allows you to get rid of arguments against your thesis quickly and then devote the rest of the paper to making your case. See which works best for you, unless, of course, your instructor gives you specific instructions on this point.

Once you have organized your notes and created an outline, you are ready to write the first draft. If possible, write continuously, without much stopping and starting. When you have finished the first draft, put it aside for a while, if possible. Then edit it, making improvements and corrections. Finally, write the final draft, and proofread it carefully.

WRITING COMPARISONS

Another common writing assignment is the comparison. Such an assignment may ask you to compare documents, essays, books, artifacts, political movements, or historic personalities. (*Comparison* here includes both comparison and contrast.) Although assignments may vary, the following procedure will be useful. To illustrate it, let us use a typical assignment, this one adapted from an instructor's manual for a U.S. history textbook:

> Based on the information in the chapter, compare the intentions and results of the Reconstruction plans of President Andrew Johnson and Congress. If given a chance, what would the results of each have been?

The first step is to make a list of differences and similarities. You can do this by hand or on a computer. In either case, your list might look like this:

Differences

Johnson's Plan	Congressional Plan
Voting limited to whites	Black men guaranteed right to vote
Pardoned prominent ex-Confederates, allowing them to hold office	Banned prominent ex-Confederates from holding office
No provision for African-American civil rights (Johnson opposed such rights)	Required states to ratify Fourteenth Amendment, guaranteeing civil rights for African Americans
No provision for African-American suffrage (Johnson opposed it)	States required to grant African-American suffrage
Ended military occupation as soon as new state constitutions created	Former Confederate states divided into military districts and governed by army
Many former high Confederates elected	Republicans dominated resulting elections
States passed black codes, limiting African-Americans' freedom	Fourteenth Amendment guaranteed African-American civil rights

Similarities

Johnson's Plan	Congressional Plan
Voters elected state constitutional conventions	Voters elected state constitutional conventions
Initially banned prominent former Confederates from voting or holding office (but see differences)	Banned prominent former Confederates from voting or holding office
No land set aside for former slaves	No land set aside for former slaves

The list does not have to be formal; it is just a tool for thinking about the subject and organizing your thoughts.

Next, draft a thesis. Although comparison essays may seem to call simply for a discussion of similarities and differences, like most other types of writing, they should have a thesis. In this type of essay most theses will summarize the similarities and differences. Since the list above shows differences vastly outnumbering similarities, the thesis statement would probably make that point. It might, for example, say, "In almost every respect, the Reconstruction plans of President Andrew Johnson and Congress were diametrically opposed."

However, the plans do contain similarities. In both, the voters elected constitutional conventions, and prominent former Confederates were banned from holding office. Both also failed to provide slaves with land. You could incorporate this similarity into your thesis statement, making it (and your essay) more complex and interesting than it otherwise would have been. The new thesis statement would then read, "Although in most respects, the Reconstruction plans of President Andrew Johnson and Congress seem diametrically opposed to each other, they suffered from the same serious flaw of making no provision for landowning by former slaves."

The next step is to convert your list of differences and similarities into notes. Although you might write directly from your list, it is easier to do from notes. In the notes, you can add explanations and qualifications.

Once you have made the notes, put them in order, and then make an outline. The first item will be the introduction. This should include the following elements, described earlier in this chapter: (1) significance of subject, (2) subject, (3) thesis.

The second element will be the body of the paper. This will contain a detailed discussion of the similarities and differences. In writing this, you can use one of two basic forms of organization. In the first, you would examine one plan in its entirety, then discuss the other. In the second, you would compare the two point by point. If you use the first method, your outline might look like this:

 I. Introduction
 II. Andrew Johnson's plan
   a. Voters elected state constitutional conventions
   b. Banned prominent former Confederates from voting or holding office but later pardoned many
   c. No provision for African-American civil rights (Johnson opposed them)
   d. No provision for African-American voting (Johnson opposed it)
   e. Ended military occupation as soon as new state constitutions created
   f. Many former high Confederates elected
   g. States passed black codes, limiting African-American freedom of movement
   h. No land set aside for former slaves
 III. The Congressional plan
   a. Voters elected state constitutional conventions
   b. Banned prominent former Confederates from voting or holding office
   c. Required states to ratify Fourteenth Amendment, creating civil rights for African-Americans
   d. States required to grant African-American suffrage
   e. Former Confederate states divided into military districts and governed by army
   f. Republicans dominated resulting elections
   g. No land granted to freed slaves
 IV. Conclusion

If you use the second plan, your outline might look like this:

 I. Introduction
 II. State constitutional conventions. Both plans called for them
 III. Voting
   a. Johnson's plan: did not allow African-Americans to vote
   b. Congressional plan required states to allow African-American men to vote
 IV. Former Confederate officials.
   a. Johnson's plan banned from office, but Johnson pardoned many
   b. Congressional plan: Fourteenth Amendment banned from office unless two-thirds vote of Congress
 V. African-American civil rights
   a. Johnson's plan made no provision
     1. Johnson himself opposed

    2. Many states passed black codes, restricting them
   b. Congressional plan required passage of Fourteenth Amendment, which guaranteed such rights
 VI. Land for former slaves
   a. Johnson's plan: No provision
   b. Congressional plan: No provision
 VII. Conclusion

In most cases, the second method is preferable. Since the comparisons are immediate, they are often sharper and clearer.

Variations of both methods are possible. One possibility would be to summarize both of the plans and then compare them in detail, as in the following outline:

 I. Introduction
 II. Main features of plans
   a. Johnson's plan
   b. Congressional plan
 III. State constitutional conventions
   a. Johnson's plan called for them
   b. Congressional plan called for them
 IV. Voting for constitutional conventions
   a. Johnson's plan: did not allow blacks to vote
   b. Allowed black men to vote
 V. Former Confederate officials
   a. Banned from office, but Johnson pardoned many of them
   b. Congress: Fourteenth Amendment banned from office unless two-thirds vote of Congress
 VI. African-American civil rights
   a. Johnson: no provision
    1. Johnson opposed
    2. Many states passed black codes, restricting them
   b. Congress: required passage of Fourteenth Amendment, which guaranteed such rights
 VII. Land for former slaves
   a. Johnson: No provision
   b. None. Opposition based on . . .
VIII. Conclusion

In your conclusion, you should usually refer to the thesis without repeating it. You should then gracefully bow out, perhaps by indicating the significance of the subject or of your thesis.

Once you have made notes and created an outline, you should then follow the usual process of writing. Write a first draft; set it aside, if you can; revise it; write a final draft; and proofread it carefully.

Comparing Primary-Source Documents

Instructors sometimes ask students to write comparisons of primary-source documents (material created at the time under study). In an introductory U.S. history course, for example, the instructor might ask students to write a comparison of British and colonial accounts of the fighting at Lexington and Concord, Massachusetts, which began the Revolutionary War. Here is an excerpt from the British description, written by the commander of the British detachment, Lieutenant-Colonel F. Smith, to General Thomas Gage, the commander of the British army (both versions retain the original spelling, capitalization, and punctuation):

SIR,—In obedience to your Excellency's commands, I marched on the evening of the 18th inst. with the corps of grenadiers and light infantry for Concord, to execute your Excellency's orders with respect to destroying all ammunition, artillery, tents, &c, collected there . . .

I think it proper to observe that when I had got some miles on the march from Boston, I detached six light infantry companies to march with all expedition to seize the two bridges on different roads beyond Concord. On these companies' arrival at Lexington, I understand, from the report of Major Pitcairn, who was with them, and from many officers, that they found on a green close to the road a body of the country people, drawn up in military order, with arms and accoutrements, and, as appeared after, loaded; and that they had posted some men in a dwelling and Meeting-house. Our troops advanced towards them without any intention of injuring them, further than to inquire the reason of their being thus assembled, and, if not satisfactory, to have secured their arms, but they in confusion went off, principally to the left, only one of them fired before he went off, and three or four more jumped over a wall and fired from behind it among the soldiers, on which the troops returned it, and killed several of them. They likewise fired on the soldiers from the Meeting and dwelling-houses. . . . Rather earlier than this, on the road, a countryman from behind a wall had snapped his piece at Lieutenants Adair and Sutherland, but it flashed and did not go off. After this, we saw some in the woods, but marched on to Concord without anything further happening. While at Concord we saw vast numbers assembling in many parts; at one of the bridges they marched down, with a very considerable body, on the light infantry posted there. On their coming pretty near, one of our men fired on them, which they returned; on which an action ensured, and some few were killed and wounded. In this affair, it appears that, after the bridge was quitted, they scalped and otherwise ill-treated one or two of the men who were either killed or severely wounded. . . . On our leaving Concord to return to Boston, they began to fire on us from behind the walls, ditches, trees, &c., which, as we marched, increased to a very great degree, and continued without intermission of five minutes altogether, for, I believe, upwards of eighteen miles; so that I can't think but it must have been a preconcerted scheme in them, to attack the King's troops the first favorable opportunity that offered, otherwise, I think they could not, in so short a time from our marching, have raised such a numerous body, and for so great a space of ground. Notwithstanding the enemy's numbers, they did not make one gallant attempt during so long an action, though our men were so very much fatigued, but kept under cover.

I have the honor &c.,

F. Smith, Lieutenant-Colonel, 10th Foot

Here is the American description, from the Massachusetts Provincial Congress:

Watertown, April 26th, 1775

In the provincial congress of Massachusetts, to the inhabitants of Great Britain.

Friends and fellow subjects—Hostilities are at length commenced in this colony by the troops under the command of general Gage, and it being of the greatest importance, that an early, true, and authentic account of this inhuman proceeding should be known to you, the congress of this colony have transmitted the same, and from want of a session of the hon. Continental congress, think it proper to address you on the alarming occasion.

By the clearest depositions relative to this transaction, it will appear that on the night preceding the nineteenth of April instant, a body of the king's troops, under the command of colonel Smith, were secretly landed at Cambridge, with an apparent design to take or destroy the military and other stores, provided for the defence of this colony, and deposited at Concord—that some inhabitants of the colony, on the night aforesaid, whilst traveling peaceably on the road, between Boston and Concord, were seized and greatly abused by armed men, who appeared to be officers of general Gage's army; that the town of Lexington, by these means, was alarmed, and a company of the inhabitants mustered on the occasion—that the regular troops on their way to Concord, marched into the said town of Lexington, and the said company, on their approach, began to disperse—that, notwithstanding this, the regulars rushed on with great violence and first began hostilities, by firing on said Lexington company, whereby they killed eight, and wounded several others—that the regulars continued their fire, until those of said company, who were neither killed nor wounded, had made their escape—that colonel Smith, with the detachment then marched to Concord, where a number of provincials were again fired on by the troops, two of them killed and several wounded, before the provincials fired on them, and provincials were again fired on by the troops, produced an engagement that lasted through the day, in which many of the provincials and more of the regular troops were killed and wounded.

To give a particular account of the ravages of the troops, as they retreated from Concord to Charlestown, would be very difficult, if not impracticable; let it suffice to say, that a great number of the houses on the road were plundered and rendered unfit for use, several were burnt, women in child-bed were driven by the soldiery naked into the streets, old men peaceably in their houses were shot dead, and such scenes exhibited as would disgrace the annals of the most uncivilized nation.

These, brethren, are marks of ministerial vengeance against this colony, for refusing with her sister colonies, a submission to slavery; but they have not yet detached us from our royal sovereign. We profess to be his loyal and dutiful subjects, and so hardly dealt with as we have been, are still ready, with our lives and fortunes, to defend his person, family, crown and dignity. Nevertheless, to the persecution and tyranny of his cruel ministry we will not tamely submit—appealing to Heaven for the justice of our cause, we determine to die or be free. . . .

By order,
Joseph Warren, President

These two accounts of familiar events contain both similarities and differences. To write a comparison, follow the steps used in creating a comparison essay. First, make a list of the similarities and differences. You can use many different formats for making such lists; here is one:

Similarities

British troops sent to destroy arms at Concord.

Differences

Colonial account says arms stored there for defense of colony.
British account does not indicate why stored there.
Colonial account: Men who appeared to be British troops abused civilians on road. This led to mustering of colonists in Lexington.
British account: Colonist behind wall had snapped piece at Lieutenants Adair and Sutherland.
British saw other people in woods but did not harm them.

Similarities

Fighting broke out at Lexington. Militia beginning to disperse before shots fired.

Differences

British: A colonist fired first and continued to fire from behind a wall until the British returned fire.
Colonists: Troops rushed in with hostility, fired first, and continued firing.

Similarities

At Concord British fired first.

Differences

British account: British only fired after colonists came very close to British troops.
Colonists: Give no reason for British firing.
British: Colonists scalped and otherwise mistreated dead and wounded British soldiers.
Colonists: No mention of mistreating casualties.

Differences

British: On British march back to Boston colonists harassed them the whole way. No mention of British mistreatment of civilians.
Colonists: No mention harassment by colonials. British mistreated civilians: plundered and burned houses, drove women in childbirth outdoors naked, shot peaceful old men dead.

Second, write a tentative thesis, which you can later modify if you need to. Third, put the differences and similarities you listed into notes, and create an outline. After organizing the paper, write a rough draft.

In comparing documents, you may find it useful to use direct quotations. You should do so only, however, when the exact wording is important to your point. Even then, keep them as short as possible. For example, to illustrate the Massachusetts legislature's claim that British troops abused civilians, you might want to quote it directly. The whole sentence reads,

> To give a particular account of the ravages of the troops, as they retreated from Concord to Charlestown, would be very difficult, if not impracticable; let it suffice to say, that a great number of the houses on the road were plundered and rendered unfit for use, several were burnt, women in child-bed were driven by the soldiery naked into the streets, old men peaceably in their houses were shot dead, and such scenes exhibited as would disgrace the annals of the most uncivilized nation.

Quoting this entire passage, however, is not the most effective way to use it. You can make your point far better by using only the most telling phrases. Here, for example, is how you might do that. In this selection the writer introduces the quotations using her own words:

> The colonists claimed that British troops abused civilians, citing such flagrant examples as "women in child-bed . . . driven by the soldiery naked into the streets" and "old men peaceably in their houses . . . shot dead."

Notice the use of ellipses to omit parts of the quotation that are unnecessary for making the point.

Once you have written a rough draft, put it aside for a while. Then revise it. Write a final draft, and proofread it.

Comparing Articles or Essays

Another type of comparative essay compares two or more articles or essays. Such assignments require the same process as writing other comparison essays. Make a list of the similarities and differences, compose a thesis, put the similarities and differences into notes, and create an outline. Organize the paper as you would other types of comparison. Then write a rough draft, set it aside, revise it, write a final draft, and proofread it.

WRITING BOOK REVIEWS

A book review is a common assignment in college history courses. Such reviews differ from the book reports you may have done in high school. A book report merely summarizes the book. A book review, on the other hand, not only summarizes the book but, more important, evaluates it. The reviewer's task is to indicate what the book is about, what the author is trying to do, and what its strengths and weaknesses are.

Reading a Book for Review

When reading the book, keep your purpose in mind. It is not primarily recreation, needless to say, but gleaning the information you will need for writing. In reading for a review, begin by examining the table of contents. It will reveal how the book is organized and often the author's emphases as well. As you read, be sure to take notes. In doing so, look for the following information, which you will discuss in your review: the main point of the book, other important points, the author's interpretation of the subject, the reasoning and evidence employed in the book, the persuasiveness of the argument or interpretation, the organization, its writing style, other features of the book and their effectiveness, and the similarities to or differences from other books in the same field.

An important part of any book review is the author's interpretation. Although history is often narrative, few historians write merely to tell a story. They usually want to present an interpretation and make other points as well. Often, they encapsulate the interpretation in a precise thesis statement, which frequently appears in the preface. Read it carefully. Besides the thesis, the preface often also contains a discussion of questions the author intends to answer and a history of historians' treatment of them. Sometimes authors also state the thesis in the first chapter, and they often restate it in the conclusion. Historians, therefore, often read the table of contents, preface, first chapter, and final chapter before reading the rest of the book. Occasionally, a writer will not spell the thesis out but simply imply it. In such a case, you, as the reviewer, must do your best to determine what it is.

Be alert to other major points. These also sometimes appear in the preface or introduction. At other times you may find them at the beginning or end of chapters. Sometimes they will appear in a part of a chapter where the author discusses what other writers have said about a subject. In *Modern Italy* by Martin Clark, for example, the author introduces his position on Fascism by describing first what other historians have said on the subject. Then at the beginning of the next paragraph he makes his own point: "The only indisputable conclusion is that Fascism was a number of complex local movements, linked by patriotic sentiment, by hatred of Socialism, and by the myth of [the] Duce [Mussolini]."[2] When you read a statement like this, make a note of it.

Organizing and Writing the Review

Once you have read the book and taken notes, you are ready to organize and write the review. Follow the general instructions on efficient writing described earlier in this chapter. Although some professional historians omit a thesis statement in a book review, it can prove helpful. As a summary of the strengths and weaknesses of a book, it can help hold the review together and can also help the writer formulate an original insight into the book. Unless you receive other instructions, therefore, include one. After drafting a thesis, arrange your notes, either by hand or on a computer. Then create an outline. Most academic book reviews have the following organization:

- Short introduction.
- Brief summary of book with a description of the interpretation and other important points.
- Assessment of the interpretation and main points and the arguments used to support them.
- Comparison of the book to other books on the same subject. Follow any instructions your instructor gives on this point.
- Evaluation of the writing style and other aspects of the presentation (e.g., illustrations, bibliography, etc., where relevant).
- Conclusion, with a brief assessment of the value of the book and its place in material about its subject.

A summary should not involve detailing the entire contents but concisely describing the subject, scope, and main points of the book. If, for instance, you reviewed *Women at Work* by Thomas Dublin,[3] a history of women workers in nineteenth-century Lowell, Massachusetts, you might note that the book tells who the workers were, where they came from, and what their lives were like. It also describes the early union movement and these workers' eventual replacement by immigrants. Your summary should also indicate anything else noteworthy in the contents. You should then discuss the interpretation.

Next, evaluate the evidence and arguments the author uses. Is the evidence sufficient? Is it relevant? Are the arguments persuasive? What flaws, if any, do they contain?

Briefly comment on the style of the book. Is it appropriate for the intended audience? Occasionally, the audience will be the general public, sometimes the educated public, and frequently historians or other scholars. If the book is primarily for historians, you can expect a specialized vocabulary; references familiar to them but not, perhaps, to the general public; and more detail than is typical in a book for nonspecialists. You must take this into consideration in reviewing such a book. Avoid describing books as "boring"—some professors even ban the word. At the same time, however, you may note whether the language is appropriate and may mention any stylistic virtues or defects the book might possess. Other aspects of the book, such as the illustrations and bibliography, may also be important.

As you prepare to write your review, try to think of other historical works to which you might compare it. Lack of such knowledge is not fatal, but if you have read such works, consider them in your review. Some instructors also require students to relate their books to other material in the course; in such cases, be sure to do so.

Once you have arranged your notes in order and created an outline, write a rough draft. As much as possible, write continuously until you have finished. Once you have written the first draft, set it aside for a while. Then edit it. Prepare a second draft. Finally, carefully proofread the version you hand in.

Writing Comparative Book Reviews

Another type of assignment is the comparative book review, which involves reviewing several books, usually on the same subject. The purpose of a comparative book review is not simply to describe the books but to examine their differences and similarities and evaluate them. Although you will have to describe each book briefly, you should devote the bulk of your review to the similarities and differences and to your evaluations, which result from your comparisons. Writing this kind of essay requires combining the techniques of a regular book review with those of a comparative essay. Instructors often provide detailed instructions when they make writing assignments, and students who receive such guidelines should follow them carefully. In general, however, observe the following guidelines:

First, of course, read the books, noting the same points you would in preparing to review a single book. Note each book's scope, subjects, and main points. Pay particular attention to the interpretation. Notice other major points the author makes. Evaluate the evidence and reasoning adduced to support the interpretation and other points. Finally, observe the book's style and any other relevant aspects of the presentation. As you read, take notes, indicating page numbers for future reference.

Develop a thesis statement. For students, this can help hold the review together. Usually, your thesis should summarize the most or least effective aspects of the books being reviewed. You might, for example, review two books on upstate New York during the first half of the nineteenth century. One deals with a town, the other with a whole region. Perhaps on the basis of these two books, you conclude that dealing with individual towns is more revealing than attempting to cover broader areas. A statement to that effect could be your thesis. Of course, you can later modify your thesis as you work with your essay.

After drafting a tentative thesis, make a list of all of the differences and similarities you can think of. These can include the books' theses, their underlying ideologies, their scope, emphasis, evidence, logic, and writing style. Once you have done this, put the differences and similarities into the form of notes. Arrange all of your notes in the order you want to use them. Then make an outline. Although the structure can vary, reviews by professional historians tend to contain an introduction, a discussion of each book under review, and a conclusion, as in this outline:

I. Introduction
II. Discussion of first book
III. Discussion of second book
IV. Conclusion

Occasionally, rather than discussing each book separately, reviewers compare them point by point, as illustrated in this outline:

I. Introduction
II. Brief description of books
  a. Brief description of book #1
  b. Brief description of book #2
III. Comparison of first aspect of books (e.g., scope)
  a. Book #1
  b. Book #2
IV. Comparison of second aspect of books
  a. Book #1
  b. Book #2
V. Comparison of third aspect of books
  a. Book #1
  b. Book #2
VI. Conclusion

Unless you receive other instructions, you may choose the organizational scheme that seems to work best. Having made notes and prepared an outline, go through the rest of the writing process. Write a rough draft. Set it aside if you have time. Revise it, write a final draft, and proofread.

QUICK REVIEW

- **In all papers, use an efficient writing process:** Make notes, draft a tentative thesis, put your notes in order, develop an introduction, compose a first draft, revise, write a final draft, and proofread.
- **In short essays,** adopt a thesis, list the arguments for and against your thesis, follow the organization recommended in this chapter, and use the writing process described in the chapter.
- **For comparison papers,** make a list of similarities and differences, draft a thesis, turn the similarities and differences into notes, and follow the rest of the efficient writing process.
- **In writing book reviews,** read the book, making notes on the contents, interpretation, main points, persuasiveness, organization and style, and similarities to or differences from similar books. Organize your notes, write your first draft, revise it, prepare a final draft, and proofread.

NOTES

1. Adapted from the instructor's manual for Jeanne Boydston, Nick Cullather, Jan Ellen Lewis, Michael McGerr, and James Oakes, *Making a Nation: The United States and Its People* (Upper Saddle River, NJ: Prentice Hall, 2002).

2. Martin Clark, *Modern Italy, 1871–1995*, 2nd ed. (London and New York: Longman, 1996), 218–219.

3. Thomas Dublin, *Women at Work* (New York: Columbia University Press, 1979).

CHAPTER 9

HOW TO WRITE
RESEARCH PAPERS

AT A GLANCE

- Choose a topic.
- Create a bibliography.
- Plan and keep track of your research.
- Find sources.
- Get information and take notes.
- Organize the paper and prepare to write.
- Write a rough draft.
- Revise the rough draft, write the final draft, and proofread.

For many students, research papers are among the most intimidating assignments they face. They are, in fact, complex projects, requiring several intellectual skills. Understanding these skills will make the task easier and produce better papers. This chapter describes each of these skills; in writing a paper, you can read individual sections or the whole chapter.

CHOOSING A SUBJECT

In some classes instructors assign subjects or provide a list to choose from; in others students choose their own, often in consultation with their instructor. If you select your own, you should, obviously, seek one that interests you, one for which you will be able to do justice to in the amount of time available, and one for which you can find the right amount of material from available sources, usually the Internet and your college or university library.

If you are struggling to find the right subject, here are some helpful techniques. First, make a list of things you think might interest you. Just jot them down. Second, thumb through your textbook or other books assigned in the course, and write down possible subjects. Third, look at categories of subjects. One category, for example, could be individuals. Make a list of people who seem interesting. In U.S. history this could include Abraham Lincoln, Clara Barton, or Frederick Douglass, to name a few from just the Civil War era. If you were studying China and Japan in a world or Asian history course, you might think of Confucius, the Chinese Empress Wu, or the Japanese female novelist Murasaki Shikibu. Another category could be groups. Again, you will find many possibilities. In U.S. history you could look, for example, at New England textile workers or Southern slaves. If you were studying European history, you could consider Russian serfs or Italian peasants. In Asian history you might look at the Chinese mandarins or Japanese samurai. Institutions are another category. These could include slavery, feudalism, and guilds. Still another category could be events, like the Dust Bowl, Sherman's march through Georgia, or the freeing of the Russian serfs.

Besides being interesting, your subject should be one you can cover in the length assigned. Students often choose subjects that are too big. In eight to ten pages, for example, you cannot do justice to the American Civil War, but you might be able to discuss how Sherman's soldiers treated civilians in their march across Georgia.

How do you narrow a topic? First, you can ask yourself what within the larger topic interests you. If, for example, you want to study the Civil War, you might decide that you are especially interested in how ordinary people lived during the war. You could then ask yourself what part of the wartime population you could look at. Do you want to study people in the Union or the Confederate states? If you decide on the Confederacy, it might be soldiers, women at home, slaves, or free blacks. You will probably find even these categories too broad. If so, you could divide the subject further by geography. For example, if you were looking at Southern women, you might narrow the subject to a single city, in which case your topic could be women in Richmond, Virginia. You could also restrict a subject by time. If the topic of women in Richmond turned out to be still too big, you could limit it to a single year, perhaps 1864. As you can see, with each subdivision of the topic, you get it closer to manageable size. The goal is a subject small enough to let you know most of the major sources, allowing you to become an expert in your own little area of history.

This brings us to the third characteristic of a good subject: the right amount of research material. The sources available to you—usually in your college or university library and on the Internet—should give you enough information to cover the subject thoroughly but not so much as to overwhelm you. To check on this, look through your library catalog. If you find hundreds of books on the subject, it is probably too large. If you find none or very few, it is probably too narrow, and you will need to broaden it. You can do this by reversing the procedure you go through to narrow it. If you find, for example, that "Free Blacks in 1864 Richmond, Virginia" is too narrow, you could expand it by taking out the year. The subject would then be "Free Blacks in Richmond, Virginia during the Civil War, 1861–1865."

As you survey possible research materials, try to find at least one primary source; that is, something written or otherwise produced at the time you are studying: a letter, for example, or a diary or a speech. Instructors sometimes require the use of primary sources, but even if yours does not, it is still a good idea to use at least one and, ideally, more. Doing so will always make a good impression. For information about finding primary sources, see the section on that subject on pages 104–106. Once you have found a topic that meets the three criteria we have discussed—it interests you, it is small enough to master, and it has the right number of research sources—you are ready to move on to the next step.

CREATING A BIBLIOGRAPHY

As you do your research, you will need to develop a bibliography, which is simply a list of sources—books, articles, and Web sites—with each entry giving the author's name, the title, and certain other information. You can begin your bibliography while choosing your topic. Later, as you do your basic research, you can add the further items.

The information and form required in a bibliography depend on the citation style you use. Although some history instructors allow use of the Modern Language Association (MLA) or American Psychological Association (APA) styles, most prefer the one described in *The Chicago Manual of Style*, and many require it. Chapter 10 describes this style in detail.

Begin by making a bibliography card for each source you look at. Cards can take several forms. Traditionally, researchers have used 3″ × 5″ index cards. With the advent of computers, however, many now create "cards" in the form of entries in a word processing file. If you do this, record exactly the same information as you would on a card, and separate the entries from each other with lots of space. As you add cards, keep them in alphabetical order. Save the file frequently. Some instructors, however, still require their students to use index cards; ask before using your computer for this purpose.

Whether in a computer file or on paper, each card should contain all the information required in the style you use. The Chicago style, used by most historians, requires the following information for a book: author's name(s) as used in the source (usually, at least the first and last names); complete title; edition if other than the first; volume if any; city of publication; publisher; and date of publication. If you use other types of sources—journals, newspapers, and so on—determine the information required by consulting Chapter 10, "How to Cite Your Sources." Write the call number or other information for finding the material on the card. If you are using more than one library, indicate the location of the book or other source. Here is an example of a bibliography card for a book:

```
E476.69
G53
1995
Glatthaar, Joseph T. The March to the Sea and Beyond: Sherman's
Troops in the Savannah and Carolinas Campaigns. Baton Rouge,
LA: Louisiana State University Press, 1995.
```

As you work, write on the card what you have done with the source so far. For example, in the process of narrowing your subject, you might have looked quickly through the book's index to see if it contained information on a certain person. Or you may have read the entire book and taken notes. In either case, it is useful to have a written record on the card. Here is an example of a card with such a note:

```
E476.69
G53
1995
Glatthaar, Joseph T. The March to the Sea and Beyond: Sherman's
Troops in the Savannah and Carolinas Campaigns. Baton Rouge,
LA: Louisiana State University Press, 1995.
    Oct 10. Read, made notes on entire book.
```

(Obviously, you will omit such information when you prepare the final bibliography that you hand in.) Keep your cards in alphabetical order. Doing so will enable you to find information quickly while you work and efficiently prepare the final bibliography.

PLANNING AND KEEPING TRACK OF YOUR RESEARCH

Many students and other researchers find that planning and keeping track of their work makes them more efficient. Here are three techniques you might find useful.

Tentative Outline

When you begin your research, you are unlikely to know exactly what the content of your paper is going to be. Nevertheless, drafting a tentative plan can help you work more efficiently. After you have come up with a topic, therefore, make an outline of what you *think* the paper will contain. Such a tentative outline could look like this:

TENTATIVE OUTLINE

The Treatment of Civilians in Sherman's Marches

I. Introduction: Why subject is important. Controversy at time of march. People are still interested in Civil War. Current discussion of war crimes.

II. Tentative Thesis: Sherman's tactics good: Helped end war & give slaves freedom.

III. Criticisms of Sherman

IV. Sherman's Treatment of Civilians

V. Conclusion

This is a very rough outline, which you will almost certainly change as you go along. It might even contain mistakes, but you can correct them during the course of your research. As you work, some parts may turn out to be much longer or shorter than in the tentative outline. In this one, for example, "Sherman's Treatment of Civilians" makes up only one of the five major sections, but in the final paper it may turn into the most important part and become much longer. As you work on the paper, you may also add or delete whole sections, but, again, that is all right. A tentative outline gives you an idea of where you are going; you can change it as your research continues and you learn about the subject.

Research Paper Schedule

With a research paper, as with any big project, a schedule can increase your efficiency. Break the process into parts and assign each one a deadline. Here, for example, is a tentative schedule for a research paper assigned in a fall semester and due November 15:

1st week in September	Determine topic for paper, including (1) Figure out general subject, (2) narrow down to manageable topic.
2nd week in September	Check library catalog and Internet to make sure I have enough sources.

(continued)

3rd week in September	Find sources and take notes.
4th week in September	Find sources and take notes.
1st week in October	Find sources and take notes.
2nd week in October	Find sources and take notes. Begin writing rough draft.
3rd week in October	Continue writing rough draft.
4th week in October	Finish writing rough draft; begin revising paper.
1st week in November	Revise paper.
2nd week in November	Further revisions, proofread paper. Turn paper in.

If your time is very tight, you might want to make your schedule even more specific, indicating, for example, the days on which you intend to finish certain tasks. Since schedules like this are for your benefit only, feel free to adapt them as you see fit.

Research Paper Journal

You can use a research journal to track your work by providing a place to note what you have already done and still need to do. Here, for example, is one entry, which shows what one student did in a day:

Oct. 5, 3:00–5:00 p.m.   Read and made notes on Glatthaar's <u>March to the Sea</u>, pp. 30–60. Next time, continue reading and making notes.

Such notes help avoid duplication of effort. You can also use such a journal to jot down ideas as you work.

FINDING SOURCES

By the time you have a manageable topic, you should already have found some sources, but you will undoubtedly need more. These may consist of books, periodical articles, Internet sites, or documents. In general, employ as many types as possible and use printed as well as Internet sources. Most instructors frown on papers based solely on Web sites; some even ban them.

Background Material

Before getting deeply into your research, you may want to get some background on your subject. For this purpose, you can read relevant sections in an encyclopedia or other reference book. The *Encyclopedia Britannica*, for example, contains accurate articles on most subjects and is available in printed and online forms. Encyclopedias, however, are not serious research sources. Ask your instructor before citing them in a research paper. You can also consult standard history reference works, like *The Oxford Companion to United States History* and the *Oxford Companion to British History*, which provide short articles by experts on most subjects.

Books

The library catalog is the single most important tool for finding books. Most catalogs are now computerized and available on the Internet, although some libraries still have parts of their catalogs on cards, usually for older materials, which you may want to use in your research. In a computerized catalog, you can use either a subject heading search or a key word search. Each works a little differently, so experiment with them to find what you like best. Also, try out different words in your searches. If, for example, you are looking for books on slave families in the pre–Civil War South, you may not find anything under the subject heading "slave family," but you will under "slavery" and "slavery America." If you want more information about how the catalog works, ask a librarian. They can be very helpful.

Finding Periodical Sources

Besides books, look for articles in periodicals, such as newspapers, magazines, and scholarly journals. Articles, of course, are shorter than books and often contain more recent research. Two important indexes are the *Humanities Index* and the *Social Science Index,* both of which cover the period 1974 to the present. For earlier material, consult the *Social Science and Humanities Index,* published from 1907 through 1973. For a computerized search, you can use the *Arts and Humanities Search* and the *Social Scisearch.* Two other important works are *America: History and Life,* which deals with United States and Canada, and *Historical Abstracts,* which covers other countries. These may be in either printed or database form. Other databases are also available, some of which provide full-text articles you can read onscreen or print out. For further information, see Chapter 7, "Using the Internet to Study History"; check your library's home page; or ask a librarian.

Internet Material

Of the countless Web sites available, several may prove particularly valuable to your research. The World Wide Web Virtual Library History Central Catalogue, (http://vlib.iue.it/History/index.html), for example, provides an extensive list of history sites, organized by topic and region. Another, more specialized location is the Dakota State University "American Civil War" site (www.homepages.dsu.edu/janke/civilwar/civilwar.htm), which has links to numerous other sites, many with documents available for viewing online (important if you are looking for primary sources). Another specialized and useful site is "Documenting the American South" at the University of North Carolina (http://docsouth.unc.edu/), with numerous documents on ordinary people's lives. Like everything else on the Internet, these Web sites are subject to change. For a complete discussion of Web sites useful for historical research, see Chapter 7.

Finding Primary Sources

Primary sources are the raw material of history. In using them, you become a participant in the historical enterprise, like a professional historian. The following are the most common types of primary-source documents:

- Laws
- Proceedings of legislatures and other government bodies
- Diplomatic and other government documents
- Reports by government agencies, including statistics
- Records kept by government agencies, including pension lists
- Transcripts of trials
- Written decisions of high courts
- Other legal documents
- Speeches, sermons, and other public addresses
- Books written at the time under study
- Articles in newspapers and other publications
- Letters, memoranda, and notes written by government officials
- Letters from public or private persons
- Diaries of both private and public persons

In addition to written materials, primary sources can include visual objects, like photographs and drawings.

You can find primary documents both in print and on the Internet. On the Internet, use a search engine to look either for a subject or specifically for documents. For example, in seeking documents on Sherman's march through Georgia during the American Civil War, a Google search for the words *Sherman's march* found the site of the Carl Vinson Institute of Government at the University of Georgia (http://www.cviog.uga.edu/Projects/gainfo/marchsea.htm), which contains numerous primary documents. Among them are Sherman's special field orders, a woman's wartime journal, other diaries, and letters.

Several Web sites have large primary document collections. For European history, "Eurodocs: Primary Historical Documents from Western Europe" (http://eudocs.lib.byu.edu/index.php/Main_Page) is useful. It contains documents grouped by country and period, ranging from medieval to modern times. A valuable source for American political history is the Avalon Project at Yale University Law School (www.yale.edu/lawweb/avalon/major.htm).

You can look at the directory, which organizes documents by period, or you can also search the whole collection. It includes the Anglo-Saxon Chronicles (an early history of England), English laws, charters of the American colonies, documents from the colonial resistance to Britain, constitutions of the newly independent states, George Washington's papers, Alexander Hamilton's written opinion on the constitutionality of the Bank of the United States, the papers of Thomas Jefferson and James Madison, the notes of Madison and Hamilton on the Constitutional Convention, federal statutes, the papers of Presidents Franklin D. Roosevelt and Harry S. Truman, documents from the German Foreign Ministry on Nazi-Soviet relations, the official report on the bombing of Hiroshima and Nagasaki, documents from hearings on the 1954 security clearance revocation of Robert Oppenheimer (head of the Manhattan Project, which developed the atomic bomb), documents related to the 1961 Cuban Missile Crisis, and material on Vietnam. For the social history of the American South, look at "Documenting the American South," mentioned earlier.

You can, of course, also find primary-source documents in printed form. Holdings vary from library to library, but here is a list of the most important types of documents:

Newspapers. Besides providing contemporaneous descriptions of events, newspapers seek to influence public opinion. Many college and university libraries have collection of the *New York Times*, one of the most important newspapers in the United States. They may have others as well. Most libraries keep newspapers on microfilm or microfiche. Reading these formats requires a reader, but learning to use one is easy.

Other periodicals. Popular and specialized magazines and scholarly journals can also be useful primary sources. A standard guide to popular magazines is the *Reader's Guide to Periodical Literature*, which has been published since 1900. For earlier periodicals, look in the *Nineteenth-Century Reader's Guide to Periodical Literature*. Like the regular *Reader's Guide*, this is a serial, meaning it was published periodically over time. Check to see if your library has it and, if so, what years its holdings cover. Another source is the *Essay and General Literature Index*, which specializes in essays, but also indexes articles that may not appear in other indexes. If you know what periodical you are looking for and you want to find where it is indexed, you can consult *Indexed Periodicals* by Joseph V. Marconi. For foreign periodicals, use *Ulrich's International Periodicals Directory*.

Government documents. Many U.S. government documents are available in printed form. One is the *Congressional Record*, which contains all speeches given in both the House of Representatives and the Senate plus a great deal of material from House and Senate committees. Official documents of U.S. presidents—addresses, executive orders, and veto messages—are published in two collections: the *Compilation of the Messages and*

Papers of the Presidents, 1789–1897, and for administrations since 1897, the *Public Papers of the Presidents of the United States.*

Important documents on U.S. foreign relations are available in *Foreign Relations of the United States: Diplomatic Papers*. Pre-1949 treaties between the United States and other countries appear in *United States Statutes at Large*. Later treaties are published in *United States Treaties and Other International Agreements* or *Treaties and Other International Acts Series.* For treaties between more than two nations, look in the United Nations' *Treaty Series: Treaties and International Agreements Registered or Filed or Recorded with the Secretariat of the United Nations.*

Diaries and letters.   Two printed sources serve as guides to diaries. They are *American Diaries: An Annotated Bibliography of Published American Diaries and Journals* and *American Women's Diaries from the Collection of the American Antiquarian Society*. Letters are also good primary documents. You can search for them in your library's catalog. Use a key word search for "letters" plus your research subject or "letters" and the name of a person you are studying.

Creating a Resource Trail

As you find sources, you can use them to find others, in essence creating a trail of sources. As you read a book or an article, look at the sources the authors cite. Add them to your bibliography, creating a bibliography card for each one. Besides standard bibliographic information, indicate on the card the book or other place you found the source. Perhaps in reading a book, for example, you find the author citing *Marching through Georgia: The Story of Soldiers and Civilians during Sherman's Campaign* by Lee Kennett. You would then prepare a bibliography card with the following information:

```
Kennett, Lee. Marching through Georgia: The Story of Soldiers and Civil-
ians during Sherman's Campaign. New York: HarperCollins, 1995.
    Cited in _____, p. _____.
```

You now have a new source to examine.

GETTING INFORMATION AND TAKING NOTES

Whenever you examine a source, be prepared to take notes. Good note taking is essential in research. The notes you take should include everything necessary for your paper. They should also be in a form in which you can easily find, use, arrange, and rearrange them as you write.

Efficient note taking begins when you first look at a source. Do not start reading right away; first, make out a bibliography card. Then look through the source, checking the table of contents and index if it has one, to see if and where it contains material you might be able to use. Next, read the relevant sections. After reading them, you may also want to read other parts of the source as well, to make sure that you have not missed anything. You may also find other circumstances in which it is essential to read entire sources, especially in order to make sure you completely understand the material.

With a book, it is especially important to refrain from beginning by reading it cover to cover. You should start by assessing how useful it may be to your research. In determining its usefulness, you may, first, want to establish the author's thesis. Knowing this can be useful in two ways. This information may help you make sense of your subject. You may also want to use your knowledge of the experts' debates on your subject (for more information about scholarly debates, see Chapter 3), either as background for your writing or in a discussion in the paper of the various approaches to the subject.

There are several ways of determining an author's viewpoint. One is to read book reviews. Several book review collections are available, both in print and online; you can ask a librarian for guidance. You can, of course, also find the author's viewpoint by surveying the book itself. The best way to do this is to read first the sections of the book where authors typically discuss their purposes: the preface, the conclusion, and the first chapter.

You may also want to use the book to find information. For this, you may sometimes read the whole book (although you should, for the sake of efficiency, follow the procedure of reading the preface, conclusion, and initial chapter first, then the rest of the book). You may also, however, use the index and table of contents to find the material most useful for your research. In many cases, this second method will be most productive. In using it, be sure, of course, that you know the author's purpose, since that will color how the facts are presented.

With any source, take notes as you read. At the top of each note, write the subject (or subjects) under which the note falls. Putting a subject at the top of each note will help you arrange your notes later on. The topic you put down, however, can be tentative, subject to change as you work.

When you take notes, try to summarize the material rather than paraphrasing it line for line. This will help prevent plagiarism. Also, avoid using phraseology and any semblance of the sentence structure from the original source. Occasionally, you will want to copy direct quotations. In your paper, however, you should use them sparingly. Generally, they should be short and used for only a few purposes: to show a person's thought or language; to prove a point by using the exact words; or to discuss the wording of a document. After writing them down, double check them for accuracy.

At the bottom of each note, write down the source. Use the author's first and family name and a shortened version of the title, then the page number or numbers. Using first and family name and a shortened version of the title will help differentiate this from other sources by the same author or others with the same family name.

If a note comes from more than a single page in your source, you may want to indicate in your notes where the next page begins. If you eventually use only part of a note, you will then be able to provide the exact page number in your citation. When you have finished a card, look it over to make sure it is accurate and clear to you. You may also want to make photocopies of every page from which you took notes. Many instructors require students to turn in such copies with their papers, but regardless of such requirements, you will often find it useful to have copies.

When you use the Internet, remember that it is constantly in flux: New sites appear, old ones disappear, and existing sites can change from moment to moment. When you take notes from an Internet source, be sure to note the date and time. Although printouts are not a substitute for notes, it is a good idea to print all Web pages you take notes from. When you do, make sure all necessary bibliographical information is indicated on each page. If your Internet browser does not print it automatically, write it on the pages yourself.

Your notes can assume several forms. The traditional method is to write by hand on index cards, and some instructors may require this. If you use this method and are already using 3" × 5" cards for bibliographic information, use a larger size for notes. Larger cards will help you distinguish between the two types, as well as providing more space for writing. Of the larger sizes, 5" × 8" is particularly useful because it provides more room than other sizes. If you take notes by hand, use a pen rather than a pencil; pencil marks smudge and may become difficult to read.

The other method is to use a computer. A laptop is handy; you can take it to the library (or archive) with you. But even without one, you can often still employ this method. For materials checked out of the library or on the Internet, you can use a desktop at home. For library-use-only items, you can often find a computer in the library.

In note taking on a computer, follow the same procedure you would for using cards. The first time you use a source, write the bibliographical information on a "card" in a computer file. Then type the notes. Write the subject at the top of each note, using capital letters, underlining, or some other distinctive typography to distinguish it from the body of the note. At the bottom, clearly indicate the source. Separate notes from each other with lots of space. Keep in mind that you will want to be able to rearrange them easily.

If you put your bibliographic materials on a computer, you will find it useful to keep your notes and bibliography in separate files. Be sure to back up all your files—frequently. Also, if you take any notes on another computer, transfer the files to your main computer, often.

ORGANIZING YOUR PAPER AND PREPARING TO WRITE

Once you have read and taken notes, you should organize your paper, although you have probably already begun this process. You may, for example, already have a tentative outline, discussed earlier in the chapter, and as you took notes and thought about your project, you probably had other ideas as well, which may have changed and developed the tentative outline. Now, however, you should organize the paper in the order in which you want to write it.

Organization

How should a research paper be organized? Although experienced writers sometimes use different plans, the familiar three-part organization of introduction, body, and conclusion will serve most students well.

Introductions. Introductions typically have three purposes: to arouse the readers' interest, to introduce the subject, and to state a thesis. To arouse the reader's interest, you can use several devices, including anecdotes, statements, generalizations, and questions. Of these techniques, anecdotes are among the most effective. Here, for example, is the beginning of an essay on foreign policy:

> In December, 2001, after the fall of the Taliban, President Bush asked Senator Joseph Biden, a Delaware Democrat who was then chairman of the Foreign Relations Committee, to draft a legislative proposal for winning the minds of young people around the Muslim world. The following month, Biden went to Kabul, where he toured a new school—one that was bitterly cold, with plastic sheeting over the windows and a naked bulb hanging from the ceiling. When the visit was over and Biden started to leave, a young girl stood ramrod straight at her desk and said, "You cannot leave. You cannot leave."[1]

Articles about foreign policy can be tedious, but notice how this anecdote draws the reader effortlessly in.

Depending on the formality required in your paper, your anecdote may be personal, as in the following example by Ronald Takaki, an American historian of Japanese descent, in a book about American ethnic history.

> I had flown from San Francisco to Norfolk and was riding in a taxi to my hotel to attend a conference on multiculturalism. Hundreds of educators from across the country were meeting to discuss the need for greater cultural diversity in the curriculum. My driver and I chatted about the weather and the tourists. The sky was cloudy, and Virginia Beach was twenty minutes away. The rearview mirror reflected a white man in his forties. "How long have you been in this country?" he asked. "All my life," I replied, wincing. "I was born in the United States." With

a strong Southern drawl, he remarked: "I was wondering because your English is excellent."[2]

Despite the effectiveness of this personal story, opinion is still divided on the use of the first person in academic writing. Before adopting it, be sure to find out what your professor thinks.

Another technique is recounting a recent event. Here is an example:

> During the 1992 presidential campaign, Democratic nominee Bill Clinton promised the American people "fundamental change" if elected president. This was an appealing message to an electorate sick and tired of the status quo in Washington, D.C.[3]

You can also use a statement about a recent event to lead the reader to a more distant historical one:

> In the United States we recently celebrated the two-hundredth anniversary of the Constitution, a document that extended liberty. Unfortunately, the bicentenary of another important document that restricted liberty has gone virtually unnoticed—the 1791 publication of Jeremy Bentham's *Panopticon; or, the Inspection House.*[4]

Although writers often try to show the relevance of the past to the present, purely historical incidents can also work well, as in this example:

> On March 25, 1911, just as workers were about to leave at the end of a long day, fire broke out at the Triangle Shirtwaist Factory in New York City.

You can also begin with a statement of fact or opinion. Here, for example, is the beginning of an article on the 2004 Democratic primary elections:

> John Edwards's advance teams like to arrange the places where he appears on the campaign trail to resemble theatres in the round.[5]

Another technique is the question, as in this introduction to a chapter discussing human origins in a world history textbook:

> Where did we come from? How did humans come to inhabit the earth? For slightly more than a century, we have sought the answer to these questions in the earth, in the records of the fossils discovered and interpreted by archaeologists and paleoanthropologists.[6]

Avoid overdoing this technique, however. Be careful not to ask questions when you should be providing information. You can also combine statements with questions. Here is an example of this technique from an essay on electronic technology and privacy.

> No one likes the idea of being under surveillance, and computer privacy is a big, angry issue. But how many people have really thought the privacy question through to its conclusion? Suppose that current trends continue

to the point that everyone is without privacy—institutions as well as individuals. Who loses, and who gains?[7]

Another alternative is to state a common opinion and then examine it, as in this introductory essay in a world history book:

> "That's history!" In common usage this phrase diminishes the event as belonging only to the past, implying that it has no further consequence. For the historian, however, history is just the opposite. . . .[8]

Beginning with quotations, either common or distinctive, is also often effective. But avoid quoting dictionary definitions, such as, "Webster's dictionary defines 'history' as. . . ."

Finally, a writer can begin by simply stating an opinion. Here is an example:

> Modern technology and the U.S. Constitution appear to be on a collision course. Supersensitive audiovisual devices, computer networks, genetic identification, electronic monitoring, and other soon-to-be-available products and techniques offer a boon to criminal justice agencies. But these same innovations threaten such cherished rights as privacy, protection against self-incrimination, impartial trial, confrontation of witnesses and accusers. . . .[9]

These are some of the common techniques, but there are others, as well. One note of caution, however: Despite the example of some established scholars, avoid beginning by baldly announcing the subject, like "I have chosen to write about Sherman's march to the sea," or "My subject is Sherman's March to the Sea," or, even worse, "My assignment is to write about Sherman's march to the sea," or, worst of all, "I couldn't think of anything else, so I decided to write about Sherman's march to the sea."

The second function of an introduction is to state the thesis: a succinct statement of your paper's main point. Professional writers sometimes imply their theses rather than stating them explicitly and sometimes bury them hundreds of words into an article. But most students will find that putting an explicit sentence-length thesis statement in the introduction works best—and many professors require it. Doing so forces you to formulate your central point and do it concisely. Such a statement helps you focus on the entire paper and avoid wandering astray. It also makes the thesis clear to the reader (usually the professor who is grading the paper—reducing the possibility of professorial irritation and a bad grade).

In most cases, the thesis should be arguable; that is, something that people can reasonably disagree about—not simply a statement of indisputable fact. For example, in a paper about Sherman's march across Georgia during the Civil War, the statement "General Sherman's troops marched across Georgia in 1864" would be a poor thesis because it is not debatable. It simply restates a well-known fact, which no one with any knowledge of the subject would dispute. On the other hand, "Sherman's treatment of civilians in his march across Georgia, though harsh, was morally justified" avoids this objection. It is also open to debate. A thesis statement may appear anywhere in an introduction, but the end of the introduction is usually the most effective location because the reader easily sees it there and it leads directly into the body of the paper.

If you have trouble writing an introduction, you are in good company. Many writers struggle with them. They are one of the hardest parts of the paper to write. Some people write the rest of the paper first and then write the introduction.

The Body. The second, and by far the largest, part of the paper is the body. There is no single way to organize the body, but here are three methods for you to consider: those focused on arguments, those arranged in chronological order, and those that deal with one aspect of the subject after another. In the first type, you list the major arguments, both for and against your thesis. Then you discuss each one, as in this outline:

I. Introduction
II. Arguments against your thesis
   a. First argument against your thesis
      1. State argument
      2. Show why it is unpersuasive
   b. Second argument against your thesis
      1. State argument
      2. Show why it is unpersuasive
III. Arguments in favor of your thesis
   a. First argument in favor of your thesis
      1. First piece of evidence supporting this argument
      2. Second piece of evidence supporting this argument
      3. Third piece of evidence supporting this argument
   b. Second argument in favor of your thesis
      1. First piece of evidence supporting this argument
      2. Second piece of evidence supporting this argument
      3. Third piece of evidence supporting this argument
   c. Third argument in favor of your thesis
      1. First piece of evidence supporting this argument
      2. Second piece of evidence supporting this argument
      3. Third piece of evidence supporting this argument
IV. Conclusion

This is merely an example. You might have fewer arguments against your thesis and more in favor of it. Or you could also reverse the pattern, making the arguments in favor of your position first and then discussing those that might be raised against it.

A second way of organizing the body is the chronological approach, which historians often use. In this format the body of your paper discusses historical events in the order in which they occurred. If, for example, you were writing about a woman in Richmond, Virginia, during a year of the Civil War, you might organize it like this:

I. Introduction
II. Winter, 1864
 a. First event
 b. Second event
 c. Third event
III. A Family Crisis: Brother Is Wounded
 a. News arrives home
 b. Reaction
IV. Spring
 a. First development
 b. Second development
V. Summer
 a. First development
 b. Second development
VI. December
 a. Conditions in the city
 b. A difficult Christmas
VII. Conclusion

Again, this is only an example. You might want to organize it by months rather than seasons. You might have more crises you want to deal with separately—or none at all. You might want to have more or fewer incidents in each major section.

A third type of organization examines one aspect of a problem or situation after another. Let us say, again, that you are writing about women in Richmond, Virginia, during the Civil War. You might organize your paper as follows:

I. Introduction
II. Daily Activities
 a. First point about activities
 b. Second point about activities
 c. Third point about activities
III. Relations with Their Men
 a. First point about relations with men
 b. Second point about relations with men
 c. Third point about relations with men

IV. Health
  a. First point about health
  b. Second point about health
  c. Third point about health
V. Coping
  a. First point about coping
  b. Second point about coping
  c. Third point about coping
VI. Dealing with Death
  a. First point about dealing with death
  b. Second point about dealing with death
  c. Third point about dealing with death
VII. Changes in Gender Roles
  a. First point about changes in gender roles
  b. Second point about changes in gender roles
  c. Third point about changes in gender roles
VIII. Conclusion

You can use other kinds of organization, including a combination of these approaches. As you work with your material, you can experiment to see which seems most logical. The only limits are logic and clarity to the reader.

Conclusions. Finally, you need a conclusion. On this subject there are several schools of thought. Some contend you should simply stop, preferably with an arresting statement. Others recommend a more formal conclusion. As a student, you will probably find it advisable to write a formal conclusion, at least one paragraph long. You do not need to say "in conclusion" or use other standard wording, but you should restate your thesis and then move gracefully off the stage.

Arranging Your Notes and Making an Outline

As you organize your paper, arrange your notes so that you can write from them. If they are on cards, you may want to arrange them on a large flat surface, like a table or a floor; writers have been doing that for generations. If the notes are in a computer file, copy them to a new file for rearrangement and save both the new and the old. Then, if you accidentally delete something, you can find it again. Rearrange your notes until you are satisfied.

Then make an outline. This can be formal, like the examples in the previous section, or just a list of topics or points you want to make. Formal outlines have one advantage: They tend to force writers to consider the relationship of points to each other. As with other aspects of the writing process, feel free to change the outline as the paper develops.

WRITING A FIRST DRAFT

Once you have organized your notes, write a rough draft. At this stage you may encounter writer's block. To get through it, just sit down and write. Try not to stop. Look at a note and write about it; then go on to the next one. Try not to worry about whether you are writing well; just get it written down. You can change it later.

When you write, you can use any tools you like: pencils, pens, and, of course, computers. Some people think they write better in longhand on paper, but most people nowadays do better with a computer. You can probably type much faster than you can write by hand, and your goal should be to get a draft of your project down on paper as quickly as possible. Also, of course, you will be able to make the inevitable changes much more easily.

As you write, insert citations for every fact or idea you use, using the form your instructor prescribes. Do not wait until later to do this; inserting them as you write is much more efficient. In history classes citations are usually either endnotes or footnotes, both of which are easy to create in word processing programs. For further information, see Chapter 10.

REVISIONING, THE FINAL DRAFT, AND PROOFREADING

Finishing a first draft often relieves students' anxiety—at least they have something written. Now, however, you will want to make revisions. To revise, first let the paper sit, ideally for at least a day. When you come back to it, you will see it with fresh eyes. Then read it through, making changes. These can range from punctuation marks to organization. You may find it useful to read your writing aloud and also to ask others to read it and tell you what they think. You may want to write additional drafts. Many writing experts recommend writing several, but the number you write will depend on your time.

Now write the final draft. Make sure it fits your instructor's requirements. When you are finished, be sure to proofread it carefully. Use your word processor's spell checker, but don't depend on it. It may miss errors.

QUICK REVIEW

- **In writing a research paper**, choose a topic of interest to you with sufficient resources available, begin creating a bibliography, plan your research, and keep track of it. Find sources using the techniques suggested in this chapter, and take notes on your reading. Then organize your paper, write a rough draft, revise it as often as necessary, write a final draft, and proofread it.

NOTES

1. George Packer, "Annals of Politics: A Democratic World: Can Liberals Take Foreign Policy Back from the Republicans?" *The New Yorker*, February 16 and 23, 2004, 100.

2. Ronald Takaki, "A Different Mirror," in Mary Lynch Kenney, William J. Kennedy, and Hadley M. Smith, *Writing in the Disciplines: A Reader for Writers*, 4th ed. (Upper Saddle River, NJ: Prentice Hall, 2000), 654.

3. Christopher C. Little, "Communitarianism: A New Threat for Gun Owners," in Kenney, Kennedy, and Smith, 547.

4. Gary T. Marx, "Privacy and Technology," in Kenney, Kennedy, and Smith, 324.

5. Philip Gourevitch, "Campaign Journal: Take This Job," *The New Yorker*, March 4, 2004, 37.

6. Howard Spodek, *The World's History*, vol. 1 (Upper Saddle River, NJ: Prentice Hall, 1998), 2.

7. Charles Platt, "Nowhere to Hide: Lack of Privacy Is the Ultimate Equalizer," in Kenney, Kennedy, and Smith, 344.

8. Spodek, xvii.

9. Gene Stephens, "High-Tech Crime Fighting: The Threat to Civil Liberties, " in Kenney, Kennedy, and Smith, 313.

CHAPTER 10

HOW TO CITE
YOUR SOURCES

AT A GLANCE

- If required to cite sources, cite every one, using the style indicated by your instructor.
- For footnote or endnote forms, use the models shown in this chapter.
- If you are required to create a bibliography, use the bibliographic models shown at the end of this chapter.

CITATIONS: WHEN, WHY, AND HOW TO USE THEM

Citations: Introduction

When you write a research paper, you must cite all of the sources you use: books, scholarly journals, magazines, newspapers, Web pages, or anything else. You may also be required to do so in shorter papers. Such documentation allows the reader to see where your information came from, evaluate it, and assess how you used it. Scholarly disciplines, such as psychology, biology, and history, vary in the types of documentation they prefer. If you have done research in a psychology course, for example, your instructor probably required you to use the American Psychological Association style; in English you may have used the Modern Language Association style. Both dictate citations within the text in parentheses. As a rule, however, historians use endnotes or footnotes because these notes allow for commentary and do not interrupt the flow of the text, as parenthetical citations sometimes do. These notes usually follow the forms recommended in the *Chicago Manual of Style*, which is published by the University of Chicago Press. This chapter describes the recommendations of the most recent edition of this book, the 15th. The *Chicago Manual of Style*, however, sometimes allows variations among forms, and professors sometimes have preferences among these variations. If your instructor gives you specific instructions, be sure to follow them.

When Should You Use Footnotes or Endnotes?

You should provide documentation for every fact or idea you get from any source. You must do so whether you quote or paraphrase. Instructors sometimes differ in the amount of documentation they require. Some stress the avoidance of excessive foot- or endnotes; others prefer students to err on the side of caution and cite everything they use. If in doubt, ask your instructor.

Which Should You Use, Footnotes or Endnotes?

In the Chicago style, footnotes and endnotes use the same forms. The only difference is that footnotes appear on the bottom of the page and endnotes at the end of the paper (or chapter or book). Since footnotes are at the bottom of the page, they allow the reader to check the source quickly while reading the text, and many historians, therefore, prefer them. Some people, however, for a variety of reasons, like having the notes tucked discretely at the end. Your instructor may prefer, or require, one or the other—or may allow you to choose.

How Should You Number Your Notes?

Both endnotes and footnotes should be numbered continuously throughout the paper (do *not* start renumbering at the beginning of the next page). For numbers, use Arabic figures (1, 2, 3, 4, 5) rather than Roman numerals (I, II, III, IV) or letters.

Where Should You Put Footnote or Endnote Numbers?

Insert the number at the end of the sentence containing the information derived from a source. If a single sentence contains material from different sources, place one number where the material from one source ends and another number where the material from the next source ends. If you cite two or more sources for the same information, put both sources in a single note. If several sentences contain information from the same source, put the number at the end of the last sentence containing this information. If all the material in a paragraph comes from the same source, put the number at the end of the paragraph.

How to Create Endnotes and Footnotes

With modern word processing programs, both footnotes and endnotes are easy to create. In both Microsoft Word and Word Perfect, you begin by clicking on "Insert." A menu will then drop down and guide you.

ENDNOTE AND FOOTNOTES FORMS

The purpose of footnotes and endnotes is to provide the reader the information necessary to find the source itself. Notes, therefore, usually contain as many of the following pieces of information as are relevant: author; title; editor or translator (if any); edition (if more than one); any larger work the source is part of (if necessary); place of publication if the source is a book; publisher (if a book); page number or other location information. The information should be listed in that order. All footnotes and endnotes use this basic form with whatever variations are required by the type of source.

This chapter provides you with examples of the most common footnote and endnote forms. For each type of source, there are two kinds of notes: the longer for the first reference to a source and the shorter for subsequent notes. In most cases, you do not need to memorize these forms, although if you do a great deal of research writing, you may find learning the most common forms useful. In other cases, you can just look up and use the appropriate form. To avoid clutter, this chapter omits less commonly used forms; if you confront a situation not covered here, consult *The Chicago Manual of Style* or *A Manual for Writers of Term Papers, Theses, and Dissertations* by Kate L. Turabian, both of which are available in most college and university libraries.

Book with One Author, First Reference

For a footnote or endnote referring to a book written by a single author, follow this example:

> 1. David Levering Lewis, *W. E. B. Du Bois: Biography of a Race, 1868–1919* (New York: Henry Holt, 1993), 304.

This note contains the basic pattern for all notes referring to books. It has the following elements:

1. The note number in Arabic numerals, which is indented and followed by a period. (Word processing programs usually do this automatically.)
2. The author's name—given name first, family name last—followed by a comma.
3. The title of the book, either underlined or in italics: Underlining was used in the era of typewriters, which could not italicize. Now, all major word processing programs produce italics. Check your instructor's requirements to see if they stipulate underlining or italics. If they don't

specify, use italics. In writing the title, capitalize the first letter of every important word.

4. City of publication: When the city is well known—New York, Chicago, London, or Boston, for example—do not indicate the state or country. When it is less well known—say, Lawrence, Kansas (the home of the University of Kansas Press)—indicate the state. If you include the state, place a comma between the city and the state. Put a colon after the place of publication.

5. Publisher: Capitalize the first letters of all important words in the publisher's name. Put a comma after the name of the publisher.

6. Year of publication: Use four digits (e.g., *2002*, not *02*). Enclose the city of publication, the publisher, and the date in parentheses. Use a comma after the closing parenthesis.

7. Page number or numbers: Do not write "page" or "p."; just type the numbers. End the note with a period.

Book with One Author, Second and Later References

When referring to a book a second or later time, use the following, shortened, form.

> 2. Lewis, 118

This is the basic form for all second and later notes referring to books and has the following elements:

1. The note number, followed by a period (usually created automatically by a word processing program)
2. The author's family name, followed by a comma
3. The page number, followed by a period

Subsequent Reference to Book by an Author of Two or More Works Cited in Your Paper

If you cite two or more works by the same author, you must distinguish them from each other in the second or later citations by using the author's name plus a shortened version of the title. David Levering Lewis, the author of *W. E. B. Du Bois*, which is cited above, has written many other books. If you cite more than one of his books, you must therefore use a shortened version of the title, as in this note:

> 3. Lewis, *W. E. B. Du Bois*, 417.

Use of *Ibid.* *Ibid.* is the abbreviation of the Latin word meaning "in the same place." If all of the information in a note is the exactly the same as in the immediately preceding note *including the page number*, it may be used alone as follows:

> 4. Ibid.

If all of the information is identical *except the page number*, the abbreviation may be used followed by the page number:

> 5. Ibid., 212.

Book with Two Authors, First Reference

If you refer to a book with two authors, your note will follow the basic model of a book with one author with the addition of the other author's name, as in the following example:

> 6. Edward Shorter and Charles Tilly, *Strikes in France, 1830–1968* (London: Cambridge University Press, 1974), 27.

Book with Two Authors, Subsequent References

For subsequent references to a book with two or more authors, follow the basic short form for books and simply add the second author's name:

> 7. Shorter and Tilly, 28.

Book with Three or More Authors, First Reference

Such references follow the form of a book with two authors with the addition of the other authors' names, as in this example:

> 8. Douglas McAdam, Sidney Tarrow, and Charles Tilly, *Dynamics of Contention* (Cambridge and New York: Cambridge University Press, 2001), 125.

When listing multiple authors, write them in the order that they appear on the book's title page (they will not necessarily be in alphabetical order). For instruction on books with more than six authors, see the *Chicago Manual of Style*, 15th ed., 650.

Book with Three or More Authors, Subsequent References

Subsequent notes use a simple variation of the form for a book with two authors.

> 9. McAdam, Tarrow, and Tilly, 126.

Book with an Institution as Author, First Reference

In some cases, an institution—a corporation, nonprofit organization, or committee—serves as the author of a book. In a note referring to such a book, use the institution as the author. All the other elements follow the usual pattern.

> 10. University of Chicago Press, *The Chicago Manual of Style*, 15th ed. (Chicago: University of Chicago Press, 2003), 211.

Book with an Organization as Author, Subsequent References

Here is the form for subsequent references to a book with an institution as author:

> 11. University of Chicago Press, 212.

Book with an Author and an Editor, First Reference

When a book has both an author and an editor, insert "ed." (for "editor") after the title, followed by the editor's name. In referring to an editor in footnotes or endnotes, always use the abbreviation "ed." Place a comma between the title and "ed."

> 12. Henry David Thoreau, *Walden*, ed. J. Lyndon Shanley (Princeton: Princeton University Press, 1971), 43.

Book with an Author and an Editor, Subsequent References

For subsequent references to a book with an author and an editor, use the form for a book with an author; do not refer to the editor.

> 13. Thoreau, 44.

Book with an Author and a Translator, First Reference

A book with an author and a translator follows the same pattern as one with an author and an editor. Simply substitute the translator's name for that of the editor and use the abbreviation *trans.* ("translator) in place of *ed.*

> 14. Andre Gide, *The Immoralist*, trans. Richard Howard (New York: Vintage Books, 1970), 87.

Book with an Author and a Translator, Subsequent References

Use the same form as for a book with an editor; for example,

> 15. Gide, 86.

**Book with One Person Serving as Both Editor
and Translator, First Reference**

When one person is both the translator and the editor, use the form you used
for translator and editor, but use both abbreviations.

> 16. Sigmund Freud, *Civilization and Its Discontents*, trans. and ed. James
> Strachey (New York: Norton, 1961), 28.

**Book with One Person Serving as Both Editor
and Translator, Subsequent References**

Once again, use the basic book form.

> 17. Freud, 29.

Editor as Author—First Reference

Some books have an editor but no author. In such cases, use the editor's name
in place of an author's, followed by a comma and the abbreviation *ed.*

> 18. Charles Tilly, ed., *Citizenship, Identity, and Social History* (Cambridge and
> New York: Cambridge University Press, 1996), 124.

Book with No Author Listed, First Reference

When citing a book with no author indicated, simply begin with the title. The
rest of the note will follow the basic format.

> 19. *Collins Atlas of the World* (London: William Collins, 1983), 132.

Book with No Author Listed, Subsequent References

In subsequent notes referring to a book with no author listed, use the title rather
than the author's name. If the title is long, you can use a shortened version:

> 20. *Collins Atlas of the World*, 132.

Second and Subsequent Editions of a Book

If the book is a second or later edition, indicate the edition after the title. Write
the number in Arabic numerals, and abbreviate the word *edition* (e.g., "2nd
ed."). For revised editions use the abbreviation *rev. ed.* after the title. Some
editions are numbered and revised, enlarged, or both revised and enlarged.
In all of these cases, simply indicate a numbered edition (e.g., "2nd ed.").

> 21. William Carr, *A History of Germany, 1815–1985*, 3rd ed. (London:
> Edward Arnold, 1987), 243.

Books with Multiple Volumes

Some books have several volumes. For purposes of citation, these fall into two types. One has a title for the work as a whole as well as a title for each volume. The other type has a single title for all volumes. Here are examples of notes for each type:

When each volume has a separate title, first reference For the work referred to below, the general title is *The Christian Tradition: A History of the Development of Doctrine.* The first volume is titled *The Emergence of the Catholic Tradition.*

> 22. Jaroslav Pelikan, *The Christian Tradition: A History of the Development of Doctrine*, vol. 1, *The Emergence of the Catholic Tradition* (Chicago: University of Chicago Press, 1971), 28.

When the individual volumes do not have separate titles In such cases, simply indicate the volume number before the page number. The note below refers to the first volume.

> 23. Robert Denoon Cumming, *Human Nature and History: A Study of the Development of Liberal Political Thought* (Chicago: University of Chicago Press, 1969), 1:213.

Books with Multiple Volumes, Subsequent References

For subsequent references to multiple-volume books use the following models:

When each volume has a separate title

> 24. Pelikan, 20.

When the individual volumes do not have separate titles

> 25. Cumming, 1:214.

Book in a Series

A book is sometimes part of a series of works on the same subject or theme. A series can be either numbered or unnumbered. With both types of series, the name of the series follows the book title, separated from it by a comma. Capitalize the first letters of all important words in the series title, but do not italicize it or put it in quotation marks. Here are examples of both types:

Numbered series, first note The number appears after the series name with no punctuation.

> 26. Peter Clarke, *Hope and Glory: Britain, 1900–1990*, Penguin History of Britain 9 (London: Penguin Books, 1997), 143.

Unnumbered series, first note Books in a numbered series use the same format, although, obviously, without a series number.

> 27. Charles C. Cogan, *Charles de Gaulle: A Brief Biography with Documents,* Bedford Series in History and Culture (Boston: Bedford Books of St. Martin's Press, 1996), 43.

Books in a Series, Subsequent Notes

For subsequent references to a book in a series, use the basic book form, as in these examples:

> 28. Clarke, 148.
>
> 29. Cogan, 44.

Article within a Book, First Reference

To cite an article or chapter with its own author, distinct from the author or editor of the book as a whole, use the following form:

> 30. Jill Stephenson, "Women and the Professions in Germany, 1900–1945," in *German Professions, 1800–1950,* eds. Geoffrey Cocks and Konrad H. Jarausch (New York: Oxford University Press, 1990), 271.

Article within in a Book, Subsequent References

For second and later references, use the regular form for a book:

> 31. Stephenson, 272.

Subsequent Reference to Article by an Author of Two or More Works Cited in Your Paper

If you cite an article by an author who has written other works cited in your paper, you must provide a shortened title in addition to the author's family name. If, for example, you had also cited another work by Jill Stephenson, the citation above would be

> 32. Stephenson, "Women and the Professions in Germany," 272.

As you can see, the form is the same as for a book except that the shortened title is put in quotation marks rather than being italicized (or underlined).

Book Published Electronically

Notes for books published on the Internet and in other electronic media should provide as much information as possible. This includes the author, title, edition (if known), publisher of the electronic version, and page, and

URL. If the page number is not available, use the chapter. This book recommends inclusion of the access date.

> 33. George Santayana, *The Life of Reason* (Project Gutenberg, 2005), vol. 1, chap. 12 , http://www.gutenberg.org/files/15000/15000-h/vol1.html (accessed October 3, 2005).

Encyclopedia or Dictionary

For an encyclopedia, begin with the title (e.g., *Encyclopedia Britannica)*; then indicate the edition. This could be either a number or the year of publication ("15th ed." or "1998 edition.") Then use the abbreviation *s.v.* (for *sub verbo*, Latin for "under the word"). Do not italicize "s.v." Follow this with the name of the article.

> 34. *Encyclopedia Britannica*, 11th ed., s.v. "Anthony, Susan."

Bible

In notes, books of the Bible are abbreviated. If there are two books with the same name—such as First and Second Chronicles—use an Arabic numeral. The chapter comes first, followed by a colon, and then the verse, as illustrated by this reference to First Chronicles. Do not put a space between the chapter and verse:

> 35. 1 Chron. 20:5.

Sometimes it is important to indicate the version of the Bible being cited. Do this in parentheses after the text, as, for example, in this citation of First Corinthians in the New Testament:

> 36. 1 Cor. 3:1 (New Revised Standard Version).

References to other sacred books, such as the Koran, follow the same format.

Article in a Scholarly Journal

To cite an article in a scholarly journal, like the *Journal of Modern History* or the *Journal of American History*, use the following form:

> 37. Michael Tadman, "The Demographic Cost of Sugar: Debates on Slave Societies and Natural Increase in the Americas," *American Historical Review* 105 (December 2000): 1525.

This form is similar to the one for books, except that the title of the article (in quotation marks) follows the author's name, followed by the journal, the volume number, the date (in parentheses), a colon, and the page number. Some journals also list an issue, usually indicating it, for example, as "no. 4." Historians rarely include the issue, even though the 15th edition of the *Chicago*

Manual of Style recommends it. If your instructor requires it, follow the example below:

> 38. Michael Tadman, "The Demographic Cost of Sugar: Debates on Slave Societies and Natural Increase in the Americas," *American Historical Review* 105, no. 5 (December 2000): 1524–1575.

Article in a Scholarly Journal, Second and Subsequent Notes

Subsequent notes for scholarly articles use the same format as those for books. As in the case of a book, separate the author's name from the page numbers with a comma (not a colon).

> 39. Tadman, 1525.

Article in an Electronic Journal

The form is the same as for a print journal with the addition of a comma and the URL. Conclude the note with a period.

> 40. Gunja Sengupta, "Elites, Subalterns, and American Identities: A Case Study of African-American Benevolence," *American Historical Review* 109 (2004): 4, http://www.historycooperative.org/journals/ahr/109.4/sengupta.html.

If the electronic source does not show page numbers, simply omit that element of the note.

Article in an Electronic Journal, Subsequent Reference if Page Numbers Shown

Write the author's name (followed by a comma), the page number, and a period.

> 41. Sengupta, 5.

If Page Numbers Are Not Shown

Simply give the author's name.

> 42. Sengupta.

Magazine Article

For material in popular magazines like *Time* and *Newsweek*, citations follow the same format as for journals except that they usually omit the volume number and use only the publication date. Separate the page number from the date by a comma rather than a colon. Here is an example (the article is fictitious):

> 43. Thomas Nobody, "Why Bush Won the Election," *News*, November 12, 2004, 19.

If the author's name is not listed, begin with the title:

44. "Why the Democrats Lost the Election," *News,* November 12, 2004, 21.

Magazine Article, Subsequent References

Second and later references follow the same form as those for books and scholarly journal articles:

45. Nobody, 19.

46. "Why the Democrats Lost," 21.

Newspaper Article

Notes for newspaper stories use almost the same format as those for magazine articles but usually omit the page number. Here's an example:

47. "Companies challenge law allowing guns in cars," *Kansas City Star,* November 25, 2004.

Page numbers are omitted because newspapers may have several editions and the editors may move articles around in later editions. If a newspaper has several sections, you may indicate these. Also, if an author's name is given, you may use that in the same place as in a journal article.

Newspaper Article, Subsequent References

For subsequent references to a newspaper article, use a title or shortened title with no page number:

48. "Companies challenge law."

Book Review

For book reviews, use the following format:

49. Peter Hart, review of *The Long Gestation: Irish Nationalist Life, 1891–1918,* by Patrick Maume, *American Historical Review* 105 (December 2000): 1809.

Book Review, Subsequent Notes

In subsequent notes, use the reviewer's family name and the page number.

50. Hart, 1809.

Thesis or Dissertation, First Reference

For a note referring to a thesis or dissertation, use the following form:

51. Michael F. Hembree, "The Politics of Intransigence: Constantino Lazzari and the Italian Socialist Left, 1882–1921" (Ph.D. diss., Florida State University, 1981), 121.

Thesis or Dissertation, Subsequent Reference

For a subsequent note, use the author's last name and the page number, just as you would for a book.

> 52. Hembree, 122.

Interview or Personal Communication

If you cite an interview or a personal communication, such as a letter or an e-mail message, the footnote or endnote should include the name of the person interviewed; identification of that person, if not well known; the name of the interviewer or recipient of the communication; the date of interview or communication; and where the communication, tape, or transcript can be found, if it is available. Here are examples of notes citing interviews and personal communications:

> 53. Doreen Maronde (retired assistant dean of humanities, Johnson County Community College), interview with author, October 20, 2004.

> 54. Nosuch Person, conversation with Vincent Clark, November 1, 2004, tape recording, Nonexistent Tape Archives, Johnson County Community College, Overland Park, Kansas.

> 55. Roderick Steele, e-mail message to author, November 10, 2004.

Interview or Personal Communication, Subsequent References

For subsequent references, simple indicate the last name of the person providing the information or opinion.

> 56. Maronde.

> 57. Person.

> 58. Steele.

Recording—Including Audio, Film, Videotape, CD-ROM, and DVD—First Reference

Notes referring to any type of recording should include author, if any; title; director, if known; producing company; date of production; and medium (e.g., videotape or DVD). Here's an example for a videocassette with no author.

> 59. *Itzak Perlman: In My Case Music*, prod. and dir. Tony DeNonno, 10 min., DeNonno Pix, 1985 (videocassette).

Recording, Second Reference

The second reference gives the author, or, if there is no author, a shortened title, and a reference number, if any exists. Here's a second reference to the videocassette cited above:

60. *Itzak Perlman.*

Web Sites—First Reference

Currently, historians use several styles of documentation for pages on the World Wide Web. This book recommends a modified version of the style indicated in the *Chicago Manual of Style*. It calls for notes to provide as much of the following information as possible: author, title of the page (in quotation marks), owner of the page, the URL, and date accessed. (The *Chicago Manual* does not include the access date, but Web sites can change frequently, and we therefore recommend that you list it.)

61. Patrick Manning, "History Doctoral Programs in the United States, 2004," American Historical Association, http://www.historians.org/ projects/cge/PhD/Index.htm (accessed December 23, 2004).

Web Site, Subsequent References

For subsequent references to a Web site, simply give the author's name.

62. Manning.

Web Site if the Author and Owner
Are the Same Person, First Reference

If the author and owner are the same, omit the owner's name.

63. Douglas Harper, "Slavery in the North," http://www.slavenorth.com/ index.html (accessed November 24, 2004).

Subsequent References

In subsequent references, give the author's name.

64. North.

Web Site with No Author Indicated, First Reference

If no author is listed, list the owner of the site in place of the author.

65. American Historical Association, "AHA: About Us," http://www .historians.org/info/index.htm (accessed December 23, 2004).

Subsequent References

Second and later references use the owner's name, as in the following example:

66. American Historical Association.

No Author or Owner Indicated—First Reference

If the site does not list an author or owner, begin with the title:

67. "The Civil War Home Page," http://www.civil-war.net/ (accessed December 23, 2004).

Subsequent References

For subsequent references, use the title of the page:

68. "The Civil War Home Page."

Two Sources in a Single Note

Sometimes you may wish to cite two sources in a single note, often because both provide the same information. To do so, use the regular form for each source, and separate the entries with a semicolon.

69. David Herbert Donald, *Lincoln* (London: Jonathan Cape, 1995), 257; James M. McPherson, *Battle Cry of Freedom: The Civil War Era* (New York: Oxford University Press, 1988), 234.

Subsequent References

For subsequent references, give the author and page number of the first work followed by a semicolon, then the author and page number of the second.

70. Donald, 257; McPherson, 234.

BIBLIOGRAPHIES

Many instructors require bibliographies for research papers. Bibliographies may be a complete list of sources for a subject or the sources you actually consulted in writing the paper. Bibliography forms are similar to those for footnotes and endnotes but have slightly different word orders and punctuation, as the following examples show:

Footnote or Endnote

1. John King Fairbank, *China: A New History* (Cambridge, MA: Belknap Press of Harvard University Press, 1992), 115.

Bibliography

Fairbank, John King. *China: A New History*. Cambridge, MA: Belknap Press of Harvard University Press, 1992.

As these examples show, bibliography items differ from notes in the following ways:

1. The author's name is written with the last name first and the first name last (with a comma between them).
2. A period replaces the comma between the main elements, such as author and title.
3. A bibliography entry uses a hanging indentation, which means the second and subsequent lines are indented more than the first line. Your word processing program can create hanging indentations for you.

Here are examples of the basic bibliography forms:

Book with One Author

Ward, Diane Raines. *Water Wars: Drought, Flood, Folly, and the Politics of Thirst*. New York: Riverhead, 2002.

Book with Two Authors

If a book has two or more authors, only the first author's name is reversed (for purposes of alphabetization):

Shorter, Edward, and Charles Tilly, *Strikes in France, 1830–1968*. London: Cambridge University Press, 1974.

Book with Three or More Authors

McAdam, Douglas, Sidney Tarrow, and Charles Tilly, *Dynamics of Contention*. Cambridge and New York: Cambridge University Press, 2001.

Book with an Institution as Author

University of Chicago Press. *The Chicago Manual of Style*. 15th ed. Chicago: University of Chicago Press, 2003.

Book with an Author and an Editor

Thoreau, Henry David. *Walden*. Edited by J. Lyndon Shanley. Princeton, N J: Princeton University Press, 1971.

Book with an Author and Translator

Gide, Andre. *The Immoralist*. Translated by Richard Howard. New York: Vintage Books, 1970.

Book with One Person Serving as Both Editor and Translator

> Freud, Sigmund. *Civilization and Its Discontents*. Translated and edited by James Strachey. New York: Norton, 1961.

Book with Editor as Author

> Tilly, Charles, ed. *Citizenship, Identity, and Social History*. Cambridge: Cambridge University Press, 1996.

Book with No Author

> *Collins Atlas of the World*. London: William Collins, 1983.

Books with Multiple Volumes, Separate Titles for Each Volume

Use the form below for listing all volumes of a multivolume work:

> Pelikan, Jaroslav. *The Christian Tradition: A History of the Development of Doctrine*. 3 vols. Chicago: University of Chicago Press, 1971.

Use the form below for listing only one volume:

> Pelikan, Jaroslav. *The Christian Tradition: A History of the Development of Doctrine*. Vol. 1,*The Emergence of the Catholic Tradition*. Chicago: University of Chicago Press, 1971.

Book with Multiple Volumes, No Separate Titles for Individual Volumes

> Cumming, Robert Denoon. *Human Nature and History: A Study of the Development of Liberal Political Thought*. 2 vols. Chicago: University of Chicago Press, 1969.

Article in a Book

> Gispen, Kees. "Engineers in Wilhelmian Germany: Professionalization, Deprofessionalization, and the Development of Nonacademic Technical Education," 104–122. In *German Professions, 1800–1950*, ed. Geoffrey Cocks and Konrad H. Jarausch. New York: Oxford University Press, 1990.

Book, Second or Later Edition

> Carr, William. *A History of Germany, 1815–1985*. 3rd ed. London: Edward Arnold, 1987.

Book in a Series

Numbered series   Clarke, Peter. *Hope and Glory: Britain, 1900–1990*. Penguin History of Britain 9. London: Penguin Books, 1997.

Unnumbered series   Cogan, Charles C. *Charles de Gaulle: A Brief Biography with Documents*. Bedford Series in History and Culture. Boston: Bedford Books of St. Martin's Press, 1996.

Book Published Electronically

Santayana, George. *The Life of Reason*. Project Gutenberg, 2005. http://www.gutenberg.org/files/15000/15000-h/vol1.html.

Encyclopedia or Dictionary

Dictionaries and encyclopedias are usually not listed in a bibliography.

The Bible and Other Sacred Books

The Bible and other sacred books are also not usually listed in bibliographies.

Article in a Scholarly Journal

Tadman, Michael. "The Demographic Cost of Sugar: Debates on Slave Societies and Natural Increase in the Americas." *American Historical Review* 105 (December 2000): 1524–1575.

Article in a Scholarly Journal, Issue of Journal Indicated

Tadman, Michael. "The Demographic Cost of Sugar: Debates on Slave Societies and Natural Increase in the Americas." *American Historical Review* 105, no. 5 (December 2000): 1524–1575.

Magazine Article

Nobody, Thomas. "Why Bush Won the Election." *News*, November 12, 2004.

Newspaper Article

"Companies challenge law allowing guns in cars," *Kansas City Star*, November 25, 2004.

Book Review

Hart, Peter. Review of *The Long Gestation: Irish Nationalist Life, 1891–1918*, by Patrick Maume. *American Historical Review* 105 (December 2000): 1809.

Web Site with an Author

Manning, Patrick. "History Doctoral Programs in the United States, 2004." American Historical Association. http://www.historians.org/projects/ cge/PhD/Index.htm (accessed December 23, 2005).

Web Site When the Author and Owner Are the Same Person

Watson, Ken. "Rideau Canal Waterway, Ontario, Canada." Ken Watson. http://www.rideau_info.com/canal/welcome.html (accessed December 24, 2004).

Web Site with No Author Indicated

American Historical Association, "AHA: About Us." http://www.historians .org/info/index.htm (accessed December 23, 2004).

Thesis or Dissertation

Hembree, Michael F. "The Politics of Intransigence: Constantino Lazzari and the Italian Socialist Left, 1882–1921." Ph.D. diss., Florida State University, 1981.

Interview or Other Personal Communication

Unpublished interviews or personal communications, such as letters and e-mail messages, are not usually listed in a bibliography.

Recording, Including Audio, Film, Videotape, CD-ROM, and DVD

Perlman Itzak. *Itzak Perlman: In My Case Music.* Produced and directed by Tony DeNonno. 10 min. DeNonno Pix, 1985. Videocassette.

QUICK REVIEW

- **If you are required to indicate your sources, cite every one**, following the style prescribed by your instructor. In most history papers, you will use the Chicago style, employing the footnote and endnote forms shown in this chapter. If asked to include a bibliography, use the models provided at the end of this chapter.

CHAPTER 11

A REFERENCE GUIDE TO SUCCESSFUL WRITING

AT A GLANCE

- Every paper should have a title.
- Make the first sentence independent of the title.
- Give every paper an introduction, a body, and a conclusion.
- State a thesis.
- Use quotations effectively.
- Write simply.
- Avoid jargon and clichés.
- Write with a degree of formality.
- Use the active rather than the passive voice.
- Write in the past tense.
- Leave out unnecessary words.
- Avoid common pitfalls.
- Revise and proofread.

For most historians, clear, coherent writing is closely related to logical thinking. Everything you submit in a history course, therefore, should be as well written as you can make it. This chapter summarizes important principles of writing and discusses writing problems commonly experienced by college students. It makes no pretense, however, of telling you everything you might need to know about writing. When necessary, you should consult dictionaries and style manuals, which are important tools for college students. Other books on writing can help, as well. You might, for example, look at a favorite of many historians and other writers: the classic *Elements of Style* by William Strunk, Jr., and E. B. White. This chapter provides you with a short reference guide, in which you can look up individual items or read in its entirety.

INCLUDE A TITLE

Every paper should have a title, and in most cases it should do something besides merely restating the assignment. It should, among other things, try to interest readers. If you are writing about the Cold War, for example, avoid a title like "Cold War Assignment." Instead, try something like "How America Learned to Love the Bomb, Sort Of."

MAKE THE FIRST SENTENCE INDEPENDENT OF THE TITLE

The first sentence should make sense even without the title. If the title, for example, is "The Liberty Memorial," do not begin by writing "The Memorial is a large building," or, even worse, "It is a large building." Say, rather, "The *Liberty* Memorial is a large building . . . " Or if you are writing about Thomas Jefferson's fathering a slave's child and your title is "Thomas Jefferson Fathered a Slave's Child," avoid beginning the first sentence with "Well, this was quite an interesting story."

EVERY PAPER SHOULD HAVE AN INTRODUCTION, A BODY, AND A CONCLUSION

This commonplace advice dates back at least to Aristotle. The introduction should present your subject, invite the reader into your paper, and indicate your point of view. In most cases it should include a thesis statement (see the next section), which is usually most effective at the end of the introduction. The body should consist of a series of paragraphs in which you make your main points and support them with explanations, arguments, and evidence. The conclusion should tie the paper together and indicate the importance of the subject and your paper.

STATE A THESIS

A thesis is a succinct summary of your main point. It should be debatable, not merely a statement of fact. "George Washington was the first president of the United States," for example, is hardly debatable and is therefore inadequate as a thesis statement. If you want to write about Washington, you could say, "George Washington wisely put his influence behind the development of national authority at the expense of the states." In this sentence, which is obviously far more sophisticated than the first one, the word *wisely* indicates approval of Washington's position. The sentence thus states an arguable proposition and is an effective thesis statement. When placed at the end of the introduction, a thesis statement will make your point clear to readers and help keep your writing on track.

USE QUOTATIONS EFFECTIVELY

Most of the time you should put material in your own words, saving direct quotations for statements so distinctive that only the exact words will make the point. For example, the sentence "The steamboat carried shoes, window glass, jewelry, and tools" is far too prosaic for a direct quotation. You should paraphrase it. Avoid especially making a paper a series of direct quotations, periodically interspersed with a few words of your own. Sometimes, however, a statement almost screams to be repeated word for word. During the 2004 U.S. election campaign, for instance, the Canadian prime minister's spokesperson remarked that George W. Bush was a "moron."[1] The comment created an international furor and led to the spokesperson's forced resignation. If you were writing about that incident, the exact words of this candid but undiplomatic statement would be crucial.

When you do use quotations, integrate them into your writing. Provide an introduction to each quotation and follow it with your comments. In 1866, for example, President Andrew Johnson vetoed a bill passed by Congress guaranteeing African-American civil rights. In his veto message Johnson claimed that the bill favored blacks over whites. In discussing Johnson's veto, you might want to quote his statement. To do so, begin with an introduction, give the quotation, and then make a comment, like this:

> As Johnson himself made clear, his opposition to the bill was based partly on racism. In his veto message he wrote, "In fact, the distinction of race and color is by the bill made to operate in favor of the colored and against the white race."[2] The bill, of course, did not give preference to blacks; it simply guaranteed them legal equality.

When you omit part of a quotation, indicate the omission with an ellipsis. An ellipsis consists of three periods with a space before and after each one. If, in quoting Johnson's language, for example, you wanted to omit the phrase "by the bill," you would write, "In fact, the distinction of race and color is . . . made to operate in favor of the colored and against the white race." If an ellipsis follows a complete sentence, use a period at the end of the sentence; then follow it with the ellipsis. Here is an example from Abraham Lincoln's second inaugural address:

> *Original:* "Neither party expected for the war the magnitude or duration which it has already attained. Neither anticipated that the cause of the conflict might cease with or even before the conflict should cease. Each looked for an easier triumph and a result less fundamental and astounding."

Omitting the second sentence: "Neither party expected for the war the magnitude or duration which it has already attained. . . . Each looked for an easier triumph and a result less fundamental and astounding."

If you omit one or more paragraphs in the middle of a quotation, follow the same procedure as for omitted sentences. If a sentence ending with a period immediately precedes the paragraph, end it with the period and follow that with an ellipsis on the same line (or the next one if all the ellipsis dots do not fit on it). Do not put an ellipsis between lines as though you were imitating the position of a paragraph. Here, for example, is an excerpt from a 1926 speech in the United States Senate opposing Prohibition, which illustrates the omission of a paragraph. The first selection is the full quotation.

> Everyone is desirous of a temperate condition. But the Volstead Act [which enforced Prohibition] has not brought that about.
> Modification of the act within the clear terms of the Constitution would partly subdue the spirit of protests and challenge now so apparent.
> Again, would it not be far better for the morals of the Nation to have a temperate condition than prohibition that does not prohibit, but rather breeds defiance, and in addition leaves in its wake a rapidly broadening trail of misery and corruption?[3]

Here is the selection with the second paragraph omitted:

> Everyone is desirous of a temperate condition. But the Volstead Act [which enforced Prohibition] has not brought that about. . . .
> Again, would it not be far better for the morals of the Nation to have a temperate condition than prohibition that does not prohibit, but rather breeds defiance, and in addition leaves in its wake a rapidly broadening trail of misery and corruption?

Finally, do not use ellipses at the beginning or end of a quotation; they are unnecessary.

WRITE SIMPLY

Despite some exceptions, most good writing is simple. Occasionally, students think they will impress an instructor with pretentious words and elaborate sentences. They are usually wrong. You are far more likely to make a favorable impression by writing as simply and clearly you can. Avoid, for example, a sentence like this:

> An analysis of the subtext of the routinized quotidian sphere of existence combined with an anodyne schema of provisional existential replacements elevates this introductory tour de force into an emerging oeuvre of contemporary explorations of the temporal.

Most historians believe in lucid writing and will be impatient with the obscurity of the paragraph above—whatever it may mean.

AVOID JARGON AND CLICHÉS

Jargon is group-speak, language usually developed by certain occupations or businesses but not shared by the general educated public. Using words like *paradigm* and *synergy* may make some people feel important, may make them think they are part of an in-group, that they know the latest expressions, but it often irritates others, including, very possibly, your instructor. Clichés are expressions, often metaphors, that might once have been fresh and vivid but now have worn thin through overuse. Among the most tiresome are "thinking outside the box," "between a rock and a hard place," "The train is about to leave the station, and you'd better be on it," "the tip of the iceberg," "Are we on the same page?" "Is the glass half full or half empty?" "Wake up and smell the coffee," "When push comes to shove," and "Walk the walk." A recent addition to the dishonor roll is "going forward," in place of the familiar and perfectly serviceable "in the future," as in "We expect a healthy growth in profit margins going forward." ("Going forward" is also usually ungrammatical.) Abstain from both jargon and clichés. Whenever you encounter an expression used over and over again, often in a knowing tone of voice, avoid it. In the language of clichés, at the end of the day, when you are tempted to use jargon or clichés, don't go there.

WRITE WITH A DEGREE OF FORMALITY

Like most academic writing, history papers usually require a slightly formal approach. Avoid pomposity, but use Standard English, and eschew slang. Many instructors disapprove of first-person pronouns, such as *I* and *me*, in history papers; others allow them. Many also disapprove of using contractions (combinations of two words with an apostrophe, such as *I'm*, *can't*, and *couldn't*). Check before using them.

USE THE ACTIVE, NOT THE PASSIVE, VOICE

In the active voice, the subject does something; in the passive voice, the action is done by someone. An active-voice sentence would say, "Abraham Lincoln gave a speech." In the passive voice it would be, "A speech was given by Abraham Lincoln." The passive voice avoids responsibility, as when someone says, "Mistakes were made," instead of saying who made them. The active voice is much more vigorous—use it in most cases. A major exception is when a writer wants to minimize the role of the person performing an action. Reporters, for example, often use the passive to report deaths, as in the sentence, "The driver was killed in the accident."

USE THE PAST TENSE

By definition, history deals with the past. Ordinarily, therefore, you should use the past tense rather than the present. Instead of writing "At the battle of Antietam Robert E. Lee *misses* his chance to invade the North," say, "At the battle of Antietam Robert E. Lee *missed* his chance." Also, avoid the pretentious use of the future perfect tense, as in, "After the First World War many European women would discover what life without men would be like."

WRITE CONCISELY

Good writing is economical. It uses all the words necessary to express the meaning fully but omits unnecessary verbiage. Students should, therefore, strive to write concisely. To do so, be alert to constructions and expressions that often contribute to verbosity, such as the following:

I think/I feel/I believe/in my opinion: In most cases, you can, and should, omit these expressions. The reader knows that the judgments are the author's. The primary effect of such expressions is to hedge an opinion, to suggest that what you are saying is *only* your opinion. You might as well cast caution to the wind and simply say what you think.

Wordy: I feel that Abraham Lincoln was one of the greatest American presidents.

Improved: Abraham Lincoln was one of the greatest American presidents.

It is/It was: These expressions are often unnecessary. The following examples show how eliminating them can make a sentence more economical and muscular.

Wordy: It is important for students to proofread their papers.
Better: Students should proofread their papers.
Wordy: It is necessary for generals to consider supply problems.
Better: Generals must consider supply problems.

There is/ there are: These expressions, too, are often unnecessary. A writer can often replace them with active-voice verbs:

Wordy: There were many battles between the Union and Confederate armies in Virginia.

Improved: The Union and Confederate armies fought many battles in Virginia.

That/Who: Eliminating clauses beginning with *that* and *who* often produces more concise writing. For example,

Wordy: I visited the museum that is located in the basement of the courthouse.
Improved: I visited the museum in the courthouse basement.
Wordy: The workers who were in the town had not joined a union.
Improved: The workers in the town had not joined a union.

Other Verbose Expressions. Replace the following wordy expressions with more concise alternatives:

WORDY	CONCISE
due to the fact that	because
because of the fact that	because
each and every	*either* each *or* every
in spite of the fact that	despite
for the reason that	because
located in	in
point in time	point, then
so therefore/so consequently	*either* so *or* therefore *(they both mean the same thing); the same with* so *and* consequently
utilize	use

AVOID COMMON PITFALLS

Here is a list of writing traps that can ensnare you. It is not, however, a comprehensive glossary of usage. For that you should consult a style manual or writing handbook.

Affect/Effect

In spoken English these words sound almost the same, but their meanings are different. *Affect* means "to influence" or, metaphorically, "to touch," as in "Her speech affected me deeply." *Effect* has two meanings. It is used most often as a noun, meaning "result," as in "Her speech had a profound effect on me." Less commonly it is a verb, where it means "to cause," as, for example, "The departing secretary of state effected a major change in foreign policy."

A Lot

Written as two words; not *alot*.

All Right

Two words, spelled this way; not *alright*.

And/or

This expression is awkward and often confusing. Choose either *and* or *or*.

Birth

Do not use *birth* as a verb, as in "Finally, one of Henry VIII's wives birthed a boy." Say, rather, *gave birth to* or *bore*. "Finally, one of Henry VIIII's wives gave birth to a boy."

Comma Splices

If a sentence contains two independent clauses (groups of words each of which contains an independent thought) not connected by any of the following words—*and*, *but*, *or*, *nor*, *for*, *so*, or *yet*—do not join them with only a comma. You must either use a semicolon or turn them into separate sentences; otherwise, you will have a comma splice. Although some languages (like German) allow such constructions, English does not because such ambiguous punctuation makes readers struggle to see where one idea stops and another starts. Look, for example, at the following comma splices and corrections:

COMMA SPLICE: The facts all seem to be correct but limited, this was a very good job for authors so young.

CORRECTED: The facts all seem to be correct but limited; this was a very good job for authors so young.

COMMA SPLICE: The textbook asserts that there were three companies of fifty men each, the article states that there were only fifty.

CORRECTED: The textbook asserts that there were three companies of fifty men each; the article states that there were only fifty.

COMMA SPLICE: He speaks of meeting with others on the way to board the ships, he even gave a time line for the amount of time it took for them to destroy 342 chests of tea.

CORRECTED: He speaks of meeting others on the way to board the ships; he even gave a time line for the amount of time it took for them to destroy 342 chests of tea.

In such sentences, the word *however* often proves tricky. You cannot use it to join two independent clauses. If it appears at the beginning of a second independent clause, you must separate it from the first clause either with a semicolon or by creating two separate sentences.

COMMA SPLICE: Before the war he didn't think he'd be afraid, however after the battle began, he found that he was terrified.

Here are two corrected versions of this sentence:

CORRECTED (using a semicolon): Before the war he didn't think he'd be afraid; however, after the battle began, he found that he was terrified.

CORRECTED (making two sentences): Before the war he didn't think he'd be afraid. However, after the battle began, he found that he was terrified.

Note: When using *however* in the beginning or middle of a sentence, follow it with a comma, as in the examples above. The only exception is when a writer uses it as in this sentence: "However absurd his statements may seem, you still have to be polite."

Commas in Compound Sentences

When a sentence contains two or more independent clauses (groups of words each of which expresses a complete thought linked by any of the following conjunctions: *and, but, or, nor, for, so,* or *yet*), put a comma before the conjunction.

CORRECT: Forty-six percent of Tanzania is forests, and forty percent is meadow and pastureland.

CORRECT: There is less information here than in the previous Web site, but it is still interesting.

CORRECT: All the plans introduced had good and bad points, and there were many reasons for their failures.

Could of, Might of, Should of, Would of

In these expressions, the word *of* should be *have*. Write *could have, might have, should have, would have.*

Dangling Modifiers

A dangling modifier is a modifying phrase that lacks a subject. Such modifiers often come at the beginning of a sentence, and the missing word is usually *I* (followed by a verb). Here is an example:

DANGLING MODIFIER: In analyzing the Web site, the statements tend to be similar to those in our textbook.

CORRECTED: In analyzing the Web site, *I found* that the statements tended to be similar to those in our textbook.

Disinterested/Uninterested

Disinterested means to be unbiased or impartial, as in someone having no financial interest in an issue. *Uninterested* means lacking interest in something.

INCORRECT: Since he was disinterested in anything outside his personal life, he didn't like history.

CORRECT: Since he was uninterested in anything outside his personal life, he didn't like history.

CORRECT: The judge was from Alaska and conducted a disinterested inquiry, which satisfied all parties to the dispute.

Enormity

The word *enormity* does not mean something enormous; it means something that is both large and horrible. The following sentence uses this word correctly:

The *enormity* of what he had done burdened his conscience.

Etc.

Avoid ending a series of items, especially a list of examples, with *etc.*

"The Web site describes many aspects of the subject, such as the people, the politics, etc."

The series above is a list of examples, but *etc.* is not an example. Even in series not containing examples, avoid *etc.* because at the end of a series, it tends to be anticlimactic.

The hurricane produced high waves, flooding, tornadoes, etc.

After the high waves, flooding, and tornadoes in this sentence, the reader expects something more than "etc."

For the Simple Fact That (in the Fact That)

Avoid these wordy expressions. Instead say "because." (The second of these expressions, "in the fact that," is nonstandard English.)

Feel like/Feel That

"I feel like this is true" is not Standard English. The statement should be "I feel that this is true."

First Names for Public Figures

Unless you know public figures personally, refer to them by their family, not their given, names.

NOT: Abraham was a great president.

RATHER: Lincoln was a great president.

Give Back

This is a new piece of jargon, which seems to mean to perform public service, as in "The company has always believed in giving back." The appropriate expression is "The company believes in providing community service."

Graduate

In Standard English, a person graduates *from* an institution. It is also correct (and the original form) to say a person *is graduated* from an institution.

> NONSTANDARD: I graduated high school.

> STANDARD: I graduated *from* high school. Or more traditional: I was graduated from high school.

Hopefully

Many writers, including many historians, object to the use of the word *hopefully,* as in "Hopefully, I can finish my history assignment on time." They prefer "I hope I can finish my history assignment on time." Since *hopefully* is an adverb (adverbs modify verbs), the first sentence literally means "I can finish my history assignment full of hope."

I/Me

Don't use *I* as the object of a preposition. Some people are apparently so afraid of using *me* that they say things like "for my sister and I," "for Jim and I," or "to Kenneth and I." Prepositions like *for* and *to* are followed by *me*. The expressions above should, therefore, be "for my sister and me," "for Jim and me," and "to Kenneth and me."

Impact

Many historians and other writers object to the use of *impact* as a verb, as in "The lack of supplies seriously impacted the war effort." Use the word *affect* instead. Say, for example, "Her lack of study seriously affected her grade." You can, of course, use *impact* as a noun, where it means a blow, a collision, or a powerful impression, as in, "Otto von Bismarck's speech had a great impact on the German parliament."

Issues

Avoid using the word *issue* instead of *problem*. An "issue" is an item for discussion; a "problem" is something that causes difficulty.

> NOT: I turned my paper in late because I was having issues with my computer.

> RATHER: I turned my paper in late because I was having problems with my computer.

> NOT: I'm having a lot of issues with my two-year-old.

> RATHER: I'm having a lot of problems with my two-year-old.

NOT: My dog is having a lot of housebreaking issues.

RATHER: I'm having a lot of problems housebreaking my dog.

It's *Not* Its Problem

It's means "it is" (the apostrophe stands for the missing *i* in the word *is*). *Its* is the possessive form of *it*.

WRONG: The dog acted as if it had found it's bone.

RIGHT: The dog acted as if it had found its bone.

RIGHT: It's too bad about your boyfriend.

Irregardless

The word *irregardless* is not Standard English. Instead, use *regardless*, which means the same thing.

INCORRECT: Irregardless of the obstacles, he went ahead with his original plan.

CORRECT: Regardless of the obstacles, he went ahead with his original plan.

Lay/Lie

Many otherwise well-educated people confuse these two words. In fact, the historian David Hackett Fischer has suggested that their common use (or misuse) goes back to colonial Pennsylvania and even to England itself. Nevertheless, modern English usage distinguishes them in the following way: *Lie* is the present tense of the intransitive verb (a verb without an object). So you should say "I lie down" or "I am lying down." *Lay* is also the past tense of this intransitive verb, as in "Yesterday I lay down for a nap." In addition, *lay* forms the present and future tenses of the transitive verb (a verb that takes an object), as in "I now lay down my heavy responsibilities" or "I am now laying my burden down" or "I will lay my burdens down." The past tense of the transitive verb *lay* is *laid*, as in "I *laid* my burdens down."

Lead and *Led*

Led is the past tense of *to lead*. Use *lead* for the present and future tenses. *Lead* (pronounced *led*) is a heavy metal, often used for fishing weights.

RIGHT: He *led* the donkey down the path.

RIGHT: She will *lead* the country.

RIGHT: The gangsters put *lead* in his pockets to make sure his body sank.

Less/Fewer

Less applies to amounts: "That tub contains less water than the other one." *Fewer* refers to things that can be counted: "Paris has fewer inhabitants than Mexico City." Don't say "During the Civil War, the Confederacy had *less* draft-age men than the Union," but "During the Civil War, the Confederacy had *fewer* draft-age men than the Union."

Numbers

When writing for history courses, spell out numbers written in one or two words. A number requiring more than two words should be written in numerals. You should write out *one, twenty-five,* and *one hundred* but use numerals for *325* and *5280*. An exception is any number that begins a sentence; write it out (or rephrase the sentence). Write, for example, "Two hundred twenty years ago, when this county was established, it looked much different than it does today."

Parallel Constructions

In a series (several items in a row), all items must have the same grammatical structure:

> WRONG: It discusses the navigation techniques he used, a time line, and a description of all four voyages.

> RIGHT: It discusses the navigation techniques he used, *includes* a time line, and *provides* a description of all four voyages.

> WRONG: The Mariners' Museum in Virginia offers a brief introduction to Columbus, descriptions of his four voyages, and the date of his death.

> RIGHT: The Mariners' Museum in Virginia offers a brief introduction to Columbus, *gives* descriptions of his four voyages, and *lists* the date of his death.

Partner as a Verb

Many historians and other writers frown on the recent conversions of nouns such as *partner* to verbs. Avoid, therefore, such usages as, "During the Second World War, the United States partnered with Britain and the Soviet Union," or "Our class is partnering with an international relations course."

Piece

Avoid usages such as "Let's take a look at the planning piece." This jargon seems to be a part of a metaphor of which the rest is missing. Avoid it by using the more concise "Let's take a look at the planning."

Quotation/Quote

When writing, use the word *quotation*—not *quote*—to refer to someone's exact words. Say, for example, "This book uses numerous *quotations* from previously unavailable letters," not "This book uses numerous *quotes* from previously unavailable letters." You may, of course, use *quote* as a verb, as in "May I quote you on that?"

Reference/Refer To

Avoid using *reference* as a verb; say *refer to*. Do not say, "She referenced an important book on the subject" but "She referred to an important book on the subject."

Reverend

In traditional usage, this title is analogous to "honorable." Precede it with *the,* and use it only before both a first and a last name. It is correct, for example, to write "the Reverend Billy Graham" but not "Reverend Graham." Many people, including historians, also object to "the Reverend Graham."

The Right Words

Do not use a word unless you are sure of its meaning. If you have doubts, look it up in a dictionary. The following sentences contain words that do not mean what their writers thought they did:

> This book is a tribute to Andrew Carnegie and his tremendous *bestowal upon* American industry.

> This provides an accurate and *simplistic* summary of his life.

> He examined different sources to determine the *legitimacy* of the facts.

> I also sharpened my ability to *decipher* between fact and fiction.

> The *reliability* of the book is very good.

> European economic troubles *aided* the severity of the Great Depression.

> This is an interesting Web site offering insight and historical significance *to* Sir William Johnson.

Run-on Sentences

A run-on consists of two complete thoughts with no punctuation between them. Correct run-ons by separating them with a semicolon or by using a period and a capital letter to start a new sentence:

> RUN-ON: He had seldom been afraid before however, this battle changed everything.

CORRECTED (forming two sentences): He had seldom been afraid before. However, this battle changed everything.

CORRECTED (inserting a semicolon): He had seldom been afraid before; however, this battle changed everything.

Sentence Fragments

A sentence fragment is a group of words that, although treated as a sentence, fails to express a complete thought, as in this example:

This Web site contains a list of topics about the American Revolutionary War, which are really links to other Web sites. Some of which I have already included in this project.

The words beginning with "Some" do not comprise an independent thought, but, like many fragments, should be part of the preceding sentence. Punctuated and capitalized properly, the sentence would read

This Web site contains a list of topics about the American Revolutionary War, which are really links to other Web sites, *some of which I have already included in this project.*

Serve/Service

Use *serve* as a verb and *service* as a noun (unless referring to cattle breeding). Do not say "He serviced his customers" but rather "He served his customers." (In farming it is acceptable to say, "The bull serviced the cows.")

Share

Avoid using this word in the place of *tell* or other synonyms, as in "He shared his thoughts with us," or, even worse, "He shared that he was leaving soon." Replace this bit of treacle with "He told us his thoughts" and "He told us that he was leaving soon."

Sight, Site, Cite

To s*ight* means to see something, and a *sight* is something that can be viewed. A *site* is a location. To *cite* means to refer to, to call attention to, or to summon (as in a traffic ticket).

Special

Use this word sparingly. It means "out of the ordinary," as in a *special* order. But it often suffers from being used in a saccharine way to mean something cute, sweet, or huggable. Some people compound the sin by prefacing *special* with *very* to describe something as "very special." It usually is not. (See *Very.*)

Subject-Verb Agreement

Singular subjects require singular verbs. Many mistakes occur in connection with collective nouns, words that denote a group, like *committee, class,* or *legislature.* In American English all of these are singular: for example, "The committee believes," or "Professor Steele's history class *thinks* it should vote on whether to have a research paper." A particularly common mistake in this regard is to call a country *they.*

> WRONG: France has frequently opposed American foreign policy; *they* see Americans as excessively moralistic.

Since France is a single country, even though it contains millions of people, references to it require a singular pronoun, like the following:

> RIGHT: France has frequently opposed American foreign policy; *it* sees Americans as excessively moralistic.

Of course, you would refer to the inhabitants of a country as *they,* as, for example, in this sentence:

> RIGHT: The French have frequently opposed American foreign policy; they see Americans as excessively moralistic.

Such That

This expression is jargon. Say "So that," as in, "It is designed *so that* it uses fuel efficiently."

Task as a Verb

Avoid saying, for example, "The president tasked him to neutralize the opposition." If you have to say something like this, say, "The president assigned him to neutralize the opposition."

There/Their

Do not confuse the spelling of these homonyms (words that sound alike but are spelled differently). *There* refers to a place or forms part of the expressions *there is* or *there are. Their* is the possessive form of *they,* as, for example, in "Their home is far away."

To/Too/Two

This homonym has three forms, each spelled differently. *To* is the preposition denoting direction, as in "I am going *to* town." *Too* means *in addition to,* as in "I am going, *too.*" And *two,* of course, is the number, as in "Two of us are going." Computer spellcheckers often miss these distinctions.

Unique

This word means "one of a kind, not distinctive or unusual." Albert Einstein was, in many respects, unique; most cars are not. Since there are no degrees of one-of-a-kind-ness, things cannot be "very unique" or "quite unique"; they are either unique or they are not.

Very

This word is often unnecessary and usually detracts from the force of the word it modifies. Use it as infrequently as possible. In particular, avoid "very special." (See *Special*.)

Whose, Who's

Whose is the possessive form of *who*, as in, "Whose house is that?" *Who's* is a contraction of "who is," as in "Who's there?"

Who, Which, That

When referring to people, say *who; which* and *that* refer to things: "Many feminists were women who had taken part in the Civil Rights movement" (not "Many feminists were women that had taken part in the Civil Rights movement").

REVISE AND PROOFREAD

Whenever possible, revise what you have written. Some people think they can write well enough the first time to avoid revising. They are usually wrong. Experienced writers know that good writing requires revisions, often many.

Proofreading is also essential. Do not rely solely on the grammar- and spellcheckers that come with word processing programs. They can alert you to possible mistakes but are not infallible, or even reliable. Spellcheckers, for example, usually fail to catch the wrong form of *its* and *their*. And grammar checkers are particularly prone to mistakes. So proofread your writing the old-fashioned way.

QUICK REVIEW

- **In writing for a history course**, remember that every paper should include a title, but that the first sentence should not be dependent on it. In general, also, a paper should be organized into an introduction, a body, and a conclusion. History papers should have a clear thesis statement. Use direct quotations, but only when they are the most effective way of conveying an idea. Write simply, and avoid jargon and clichés. At the same time, employ a degree of formality. Whenever possible, write in the active rather than the passive voice, and use the past tense. Write concisely, and steer clear of common pitfalls. Before turning a paper in, revise and proofread it carefully.

NOTES

1. Elizabeth Bumiller, "Bush, Visiting Canada, Aims to Smooth Ruffled Relations, *New York Times,* http://www.nytimes.com/2004/12/01/politics/01prexy.html.
2. Andrew Johnson to the Senate of the United States, March 27, 1866, in *A Compilation of the Messages and Papers of the President*, ed. James D. Richardson (Project Gutenberg, 2004), vol. 6, sect. 2, http://www.gutenberg.org/dirs/1/2/7/5/12755/12755.txt.
3. Congressional Record, 69th Congress, 1st Session.

CHAPTER 12

PLAGIARISM AND HOW TO AVOID IT

AT A GLANCE

- Plagiarism is using someone else's work without giving credit.
- It includes wording, sentence structure, and organization.
- Students who copy a passage and change a few words are plagiarizing.
- Good note-taking techniques can help avoid plagiarism.
- Cite the sources of all ideas and information you use.

Plagiarism is a serious academic offence. Besides being dishonest, it may lead to severe penalties, including a zero on the assignment, an F in the course, a permanent mark on your academic record, or even expulsion from your college or university.

Plagiarism means using someone else's work and representing all or part of it as your own. To avoid plagiarism, you must not copy anything written by someone else unless you put it in quotation marks and give the source. Prohibited copying includes wording, sentence structure, and organization. If you copy, you cannot avoid plagiarism by citing the source. You must enclose the copied material in quotation marks (and also, of course, indicate the source).

This prohibition means that you must also avoid taking a sentence written by someone else and changing a few words here and there. Inexperienced students sometimes do this, often altering the words that give a sentence its complexity. Here, for example, is a description of the Aztec city Teotihuacan from a world history textbook:

> Meanwhile, in the valley of Mexico, another civilization was coalescing, dominating the lands near it, and finally creating a substantial empire.[1]

A student copying this sentence and changing a few words might write

> In the valley of Mexico another civilization was being formed, which dominated the lands near it and finally created a substantial empire.

The student has left out *meanwhile,* changed *coalescing* to *being formed,* and altered slightly the structure of the sentence. Despite these changes, the new version is too close to the original, even though it is inferior. It is copying, and it is plagiarism.

How do you avoid plagiarism? First, do not copy material from a Web page or e-mail message and paste it into your writing. Second, follow good note-taking techniques. There are two schools of thought about how to do this, each with its own adherents. One recommends paraphrasing as you take notes. When you find information that might be useful, write it in your notes, using your own words. After doing so, check your notes against the original to make sure you did not copy. (Of course, if you intend to use a direct quotation, you must copy it exactly and surround it with quotation marks.)

The other believes in taking down direct quotations, using quotation marks. Then when you write, you paraphrase the quotations found in your notes. You then compare your paraphrases with the originals to make sure that they are not too close. Students who do research should ask their instructors what they recommend. Whichever one you use, be careful.

Finally, give credit for information and ideas that you get from any source whatsoever. If you did not think it up yourself, you must tell the reader where you got it, using approved citation forms. This rule applies first to information. For example, in the book *Psychotherapy in the Third Reich,* Geoffrey Cocks says that the prominent German psychotherapist Gustav Richard Heyer was a Hitler supporter.[2] If you had found that information in Cocks's book and you used it in a paper, you should have cited the source. This rule also applies to ideas. Cocks, for example, argues that despite the cost to Jewish psychotherapists, the Nazi regime produced some benefits for the profession of psychotherapy.[3] If you wanted to make this point yourself, you would have to cite Cocks's book.

QUICK REVIEW

• **To avoid plagiarism**, do not copy the wording, sentence structure, or organization of somebody else's material—it is not enough simply to change a few words. In doing research, take notes carefully to avoid allowing direct quotations to slip unintentionally into your work. And whether using direct quotations or not, indicate the sources of all ideas and information you get from material produced by others.

NOTES

1. Howard Spodek, *The World's History* (Upper Saddle River, NJ: Prentice Hall, 2001), 97.

2. Geoffrey Cocks, *Psychotherapy in the Third Reich* (New York: Oxford University Press, 1985), 61.

3. Cocks, 248.

CREDITS

Page 15: AP Wide World Photos; page 41: Image Works/Mary Evans Picture Library Ltd; page 42: Francisco Goya, "Execution of the Madrilenos on May 3, 1808," 1814, oil on canvas, 8' 8 3/4" x 11' 3 3/4," Museo del Prado, Madrid; page 43: Courtesy of the Library of Congress; page 44: (top) Courtesy of the Library of Congress, (bottom) Courtesy of the Library of Congress; page 45: (top and bottom) Ria Novosti/Moscow Photobank; page 47: Columbia Pictures Corp.

INDEX

A

Active voice, 140
Adams, John, 28
affect, effect, 142
Albion's Seed: Four British Folkways in America (Fischer), 12
all right, alright, 142
a lot, alot, 142
America: History and Life, 72, 103
The American Experience, 46
American Historical Association, 11
American Psychological Association (APA) style, 99, 117
Americans (Countryman), 12
American Sphinx (Ellis), 7
American West, 7
and/or, 143
ANGEL, 65
Anthologies, 38
Arabic numerals, in notetaking, 33
Articles, 39
  bibliographies for, 134
  citing, 125, 126–28
  comparing, 92
  newspaper, 128
Arts and humanities search, 72
Ask.com, 70
Assignments, group project, 54–55
Author, of web site, 68

B

Background material, 102–3
Ballard, Martha, 13, 18
Bartlett's Familiar Quotations, 73
Beesley, David, 19
Bible
  bibliographies for, 134
  citing, 126
Bibliographies, 108, 131–35
  article in book, 133
  article in scholarly journal, 134

Bible, 134
  book, second or later edition, 133
  book in a series, 134
  book published electronically, 134
  book review, 134
  book with author and editor, 132
  book with author and translator, 132
  book with editor as author, 133
  book with institution as author, 132
  book with multiple volumes, 133
  book with one author, 132
  book with one person serving as editor and translator, 133
  book with three or more authors, 132
  book with two authors, 132
  card, 100
  creating, 99–100
  encyclopedia or dictionary, 134
  interview or personal communication, 135
  magazine articles, 134
  newspaper articles, 134
  recording, 135
  thesis or dissertation, 135
  web sites, 135
birth, 143
The Birth of a Nation, 48
Blackboard, 65
Body
  of essay, 137
  of research paper, 112–14
Book reviews, 92–96
  bibliographies for, 134
  book selection, 92–93
  citing, 128
  comparative, 94–96
  organizing, 93–94
Books, 103. *See also* Citations
  bibliographies for, 132–34
  citing, 119–26
  study of, 38–40
Bury, J.B., 17

C

Caption, on map, 34
Carpetbaggers, 16
Cause-and-effect relationships, 24
The Chicago Manual of Style, 99, 118, 119
China: A New History (Fairbank), 12
Chronology, 24, 29
Citations
    article in electronic journal, 127
    article in scholarly journal, 126–27
    article within a book, first reference, 125
    article within a book, subsequent
        references, 125
    Bible, 126
    book published electronically, 125–26
    book review, 128
    book with author and translator, first
        reference, 122
    book with author and translator,
        subsequent reference, 122
    book with no author, first reference, 123
    book with no author, subsequent
        references, 123
    book with one author, first reference, 119–10
    book with one author, second and later
        references, 120
    book with one person serving as author
        and translator, first reference, 123
    book with one person serving as author
        and translator, subsequent
        references, 123
    books in a series, 124–25
    books with author and editor, first
        reference, 122
    books with author and editor, subsequent
        reference, 122
    books with institution as author, first
        reference, 121–22
    books with multiple volumes, 124
    books with organization as author,
        subsequent reference, 121–22
    books with three or more authors, first
        reference, 121
    books with three or more authors,
        subsequent reference, 121
    books with two authors, first reference, 121
    books with two authors, subsequent
        reference, 121
    editor as author - first reference, 123
    encyclopedia or dictionary, 126
    footnotes *versus* endnotes, 118–19
    interview or personal communication, 129
    introduction, 117–18
    magazine article, 127–28
    newspaper article, 128
    notes, 118
    recordings, 129–30
    second and subsequent editions
        of book, 123
    of sources, 114–35
    subsequent references to article by author
        of two or more works cited, 125
    subsequent reference to book by author
        of two or more works cited in paper,
        120–21
    thesis or dissertation, 128–29
    web sites, 130–31
cite, sight, site, 150
*City of Eros: New York City, Prostitution, and
    the Commercialization of Sex*
    (Gilfoyle), 18
Civil War, 11, 16, 27
Class, study of, 19
Classmates, sensitivity toward, 52
Class participation, effective, 50–55
    discussions, 51–52
    group projects, 54–55
    presentations, 52–54
Clichés, avoiding, 140
Cold War, 7, 15
Columbia Encyclopedia, 73
Commas in compound sentences, 144
Comma splices, 143–44
Comparative book reviews, 94–96
Comparison and contrast questions, 60
Comparisons
    of articles or essays, 92
    of primary-source documents, 88–92
    writing, 84–92
*Compilation of the Messages and Papers of the
    Presidents*, 105–6
Compound sentences, commas in, 144
Computers, notetaking with, 34
Conciseness, of writing, 141–42
Conclusions
    of essay, 137
    of research paper, 114
Congressional Record, 105
Conte, Christopher A., 19
Conversational tone, in presentations, 54
could of, might of, should of, would of, 144
Countryman, Edward, 7, 12
Course materials, 57
Crew, David, 18
Critical thinking, 30
    about discussions, 51–52

Crow's Range: an Environmental History of the Sierra Nevada (Beesley), 19
Cunfer, Geoff, 19

D

Dangling modifiers, 144
Databases, Internet, 71–73
  America: History and Life, 72
  arts and humanities search, 72
  dissertation abstracts, 72
  expanded academic ASAP, 71
  historical abstracts, 71–72
  humanities index, 72
  JSTOR, 71
  PROQUEST, 71
  research navigator, 73
  RLG union catalog, 72–73
  social sciences index, 72
  social scisearch, 72
Deadlines, for group projects, 55
Dead Sea Scrolls, 14
Debates, historians and, 15–17
Dictionary
  bibliographies for, 134
  citing, 126
  usage pitfalls, 149
Differences and similarities, writing, 84–85, 90, 91
"Digital History" web site, 76
Discussions, 51–52
  critical thinking about, 51–52
  participation in, 51
  preparation for, 51
  sensitivity toward classmates, 52
disinterested, uninterested, 144–45
Dissertation
  abstracts, 72
  bibliographies for, 135
  citing, 128–29
Drafting
  short papers, 81–82
  thesis, 80
Dublin, Thomas, 18
Du Bois, W.E.B., 12
Dust Bowl: The Southern Plains in the 1930s (Worster), 19

E

Effective study
  of fiction, 40
  of films and videotapes, 46–48
  of historical novels, 40
  of history, 21–49
  important points, 23–24
  of interpretive essays and books, 38–40
  of lectures, 31–34
  of maps, 34–36
  of paintings, photographs, and graphic materials, 40–46
  of primary-source documents, 36–38
  memory, use of, 24–25
  of textbooks, 26–31
  principles of, 23–25
  time management, 25
Ellipsis, 138, 139
Ellis, Joseph, 7
Elvin, Mark, 19
E-mail, effective use of, 65–67
Encyclopedia
  bibliographies for, 134
  citing, 126
Encyclopedia Britannica, 73, 103
Encyclopedias, online, 73
Endnotes, 131
  article in electronic journal, 127
  article in scholarly journal, 126–27
  article within a book, first reference, 125
  article within a book, subsequent references, 125
  Bible, 126
  book published electronically, 125–26
  book review, 128
  book with author and editor, first reference, 122
  book with author and editor, subsequent reference, 122
  book with author and translator, first reference, 122
  book with author and translator, subsequent reference, 122
  book with institution as author, first reference, 121–22
  book with no author listed, first reference, 123
  book with no author listed, subsequent references, 123
  book with one author, first reference, 119–20
  book with one author, second and later references, 120
  book with organization as author, subsequent, 122
  book with person serving as editor and translator, first reference, 123
  book with three or more authors, first reference, 121
  book with three or more authors, subsequent references, 121

book with two authors, first reference, 121
book with two authors, subsequent
references, 121
books in a series, 124–25
books in a series, subsequent note, 125
books with multiple volumes, 124
books with multiple volumes, subsequent
references, 124
editor as author - first reference, 123
encyclopedia or dictionary, 126
footnotes *versus*, 118–19
forms of, 119–31
interview or personal communication, 129
magazine article, 127–28
newspaper article, 128
numbering, 115
recording, 129–30
second or subsequent editions of book, 123
subsequent reference to book by author of
two or more works, 120–21
subsequent references to article, 125
thesis or dissertation, 128–29
two sources in single note, 131
web sites, 130–31
enormity, 145
Essay and General Literature Index, 105
Essays
comparing, 92
short, 83–84
etc., 145
Evaluation, of material, 31
Evans, Richard, 18
Evidence, 13–15, 39
reliability of, 14–15
Expanded Academic ASAP, 71

F

Facts, 23–24
Fairbank, John King, 12
Faust, Drew Gilpin, 11
feel like, feel that, 145
fewer, less, 148
Fiction, study of, 40
Films, study of, 46–48
Final draft
of research paper, 115
of short paper, 83
First draft
of research paper, 115
of short papers, 81–82
Fischer, David Hackett, 12
Fischer, Fritz, 7
Footnotes, 131

article in electronic journal, 127
article in scholarly journal, 126–27
article within a book, first reference, 125
article within a book, subsequent
references, 125
Bible, 126
book published electronically, 125–26
book review, 128
book with author and editor, first
reference, 122
book with author and editor, subsequent
reference, 122
book with author and translator, first
reference, 122
book with author and translator,
subsequent reference, 122
book with institution as author, first
reference, 121–22
book with no author listed, first
reference, 123
book with no author listed, subsequent
references, 123
book with one author, first reference,
119–20
book with one author, second and later
references, 120
book with organization as author,
subsequent, 122
book with person serving as editor and
translator, first reference, 123
book with person serving as editor and
translator, subsequent references, 123
book with three or more authors, first
reference, 121
book with three or more authors,
subsequent references, 121
book with two authors, first reference, 121
book with two authors, subsequent
references, 121
books in a series, 124–25
books in a series, subsequent note, 125
books with multiple volumes, 124
books with multiple volumes, subsequent
references, 124
editor as author - first reference, 123
encyclopedia or dictionary, 126
endnotes *versus*, 118–19
forms of, 119–31
interview or personal
communication, 129
magazine article, 127–28
newspaper article, 128

numbering, 115
recording, 129–30
second or subsequent editions of book, 123
subsequent references to article, 125
subsequent reference to book by author of
two or more works, 120–21
thesis or dissertation, 128–29
two sources in single note, 131
web sites, 130–31
Formality, degree of, 140
Forrest Gump, 48
for the simple fact that (in the fact that), 145

G

Gaddis, John Lewis, 7
Gilfoyle, Timothy J., 18
give back, 145
Google, 69, 104
Government documents, 105–6
Goya, Francisco de, 41, 42
graduate, 146
Grammatical errors, correcting, 82
Graphic materials, study of, 40–46
Group projects, 54–55
assignment of, 54–55
deadlines, establishing, 55
organization of, 54
public presentations, rehearsing, 55

H

Henry, Patrick, 54
Herodotus, 17
High Beam Research, 74
Highland Sanctuary: Environmental History in Tanzania's Usambara Mountains (Conte), 19
Highlighting
of information, 23–24
of textbooks, 26
Hill, Christopher, 7
Historians, 9–20
evidence and, 13–15
functions of, 11–12
interpretations and debates and, 15–17
purposes of, 10–11
research and writing, 12–13
Historical abstracts, 71–72
Historical knowledge, 22
Historical novels, study of, 40
Historical significance, 63
Historical Text Archive, 75
History

defined, 6–5
Internet, use of, 64–77
method of study, 21–49
reason for study, 3–8
recent approaches in, 17–20
writing short papers for, 78–96
History web sites, 75–77
Hitler, Adolf, 5, 14, 15
hopefully, 146
Humanities Index, 72, 103

I

I, me, 146
Identification questions, 62–63
Illustrations, in presentations, 54
impact, 146
Important points
of lecture, 32
on tests, 56–57
in textbooks, 27–29
Indexed Periodicals (Marconi), 105
Information, gathering, 106–8
Internet, 14
databases on, 71–73
e-mail, effective use of, 65–67
finding material on, 69–77
history course, use in, 65
history web sites, 75–77
library catalogs, 74
material, finding, 103–4
online reference materials, 73–74
publishers' web sites, 75
search engines, 69–71
use of, 64–77
Interpretations, historians and, 15–17
Interpretive essays, study of, 38–40
Interview
bibliographies for, 135
citing, 129
Introduction
for citations, 117–18
of paper, 83, 137
of research papers, 109–12
irregardless, 147
issues, 146–47
its, it's, 147

J

Jargon, avoiding, 140
Jefferson, Thomas, 7, 28
JFK, 48
Johnson, Paul, 18

Journal, research, 102
JSTOR, 71

K

King Charles I, 7
Kujau, Konrad, 15

L

Laslett, Peter, 10
lay, lie, 147
lead, led, 147
Lectures
    effective notetaking, 32–34
    important points in, 32
    notes, study of, 34
    study of, 31–34
Lee, Russell, 43
Legend, of map, 34
Lenin, Vladimir Ilyich, 43, 46
less, fewer, 148
Lewis, David Levering, 12
Library catalogs, 74
Library of Congress, 75
Limerick, Patricia, 7
Lincoln, Abraham, 10, 27
Lincoln at Gettysburg (Wills), 11
Lombard, Anne S., 19
Long-answer essay questions, 59–62
Long-time memory, 24

M

Magazine article, citing, 127–28
*Making Manhood: Growing Up Male in
    Colonial New England* (Lombard), 19
The Making of the English Working Class
    (Thompson), 18
The Making of the Modern Family (Shorter), 18
*A Manual for Writers of Term Papers, Theses,
    and Dissertations* (Turabian), 119
Maps, 34–36
    caption, 34
    legend, 34
    title of, 34
Marxism, 19
Matching questions, 63
Material, textbook
    effective learning techniques, 29–31
    surveying, 26
me, I, 146
Memorization, of speeches, 53
Memory, 24–25
    aids for, 30
    long-time, 24

overlearning, 25
    process material, 24–25
    review, 25
    sensory, 24
    short-term, 24
    time management, 25
A Midwife's Tale (Ballard), 13
might of, could of, should of, would of, 144
Modern Language Association (MLA) style,
    99, 117
*Moorlands of England and Wales: An
    Environmental History 8000 BC to AD
    2000* (Simmons), 19
MSN, 70
Multiple-choice questions, 63

N

Napoleon, 5
Nash, Gary, 7
New Era, 5
Newspapers, 105
    article, citing, 128
New Western historians, 7
New York Times, 105
Notecards, 108
    for presentations, 53–54
Notes
    arranging, 114
    for short papers, 79–80
Notetaking, 106–8
    Arabic numerals in, 33
    during lectures, 32–34
    on primary-source documents, 37
    Roman numerals in, 33
    sample, 32–33
    with computers, 34
Numbering, of endnotes and footnotes, 115
Numbers, 148

O

Online reference materials, 73–74
*On the Great Plains: Agriculture and
    Environment* (Cunfer), 19
Organization
    for presentations, 52–53
    of group projects, 54
    of material for tests, 57–58
    for short paper, 80–81
    of research papers, 109–14
    of reviews, 93–94
Outline, 86–87, 95
    of research paper, 114
    tentative, 101

Overlearning, 25
The Oxford Companion, 103
Oxford Companion to British History, 103
Oxford Companion to United States History, 103
Oxford English Dictionary, 38

P

Paintings, study of, 40–46
Parallel constructions, 148
Participation. *See also* Class participation, effective
    in discussions, 51
partner, as verb, 148
Passive voice, 140
Past tense, of verbs, 140–41
Periodicals, 105
    finding, 103
Personal communication
    bibliographies for, 135
    citing, 129
Personal history, 4
Photographs, study of, 40–46
piece, 148
Pitfalls in writing, avoiding, 142–52
    affect/effect, 142
    all right, 142
    and/or, 143
    birth, 143
    comma in compound sentences, 144
    comma splices, 143–44
    could of, might of, should of, would of, 144
    dangling modifiers, 144
    dictionary usage, 149
    disinterested/uninterested, 144–45
    enormity, 145
    etc., 145
    feel like/feel that, 145
    first names for public figures, 145
    give back, 145
    graduate, 146
    hopefully, 146
    I/me, 146
    impact, 146
    irregardless, 147
    issues, 146–47
    it's/its, 147
    lay/lie, 147
    lead/led, 147
    less/fewer, 148
    a lot, 142
    numbers, 148
    parallel constructions, 148
    partner as a verb, 148
    piece, 148
    quotation/quote, 149
    reference/refer to, 149
    reverend, 149
    run-on sentences, 149–50
    sentence fragments, 150
    serve/service, 150
    share, 150
    sight, site, cite, 150
    for the simple fact that (in the fact that), 145
    special, 150
    subject-verb agreement, 151
    such that, 151
    task as verb, 151
    there/their, 151
    to/too/two, 151
    unique, 152
    very, 152
    who, which, that, 152
    whose, who's, 152
Plagiarism, avoiding, 154–56
PowerPoint presentation, 53
Preface, 39
Preparation
    for discussions, 51
    for presentations, 53–54
    for tests, 58
    of research papers, 109–14
Presentations, 52–54
    conversational tone in, 54
    notecards for, 53–54
    organization for, 52–53
    PowerPoint, 53
    preparation for, 53–54
    public, 55
Primary-source documents
    comparing, 88–92
    finding, 104–6
    study of, 36–38
Proofreading, 115, 152
PROQUEST, 71
Publication date, 39
Public figures, first names for, 145
Public presentations, rehearsing, 55
Publisher's web sites, 75
Pulitzer Prize, 11

Q

Questions, answering, 59–63
    comparison and contrast, 60
    identification, 62–63
    long-answer essay, 59–62
    matching, 63

multiple-choice, 63
true-false, 63
quotation, quote, 149
Quotations, effective usage of, 138–39
Quoting, passages, 91

R

Reader's Guide to Periodical Literature, 105
Rebuttal of arguments, 83
Reconstruction, 11, 16, 27
Recordings
    bibliographies for, 135
    citing, 129–30
Red, White, and Black (Nash), 7
"Redeemers," 16
reference, refer to, 149
Reference guide for writing, 136–53
    body, 137
    conciseness, 141–42
    conclusion, 137
    degree of formality, 140
    first sentence, 137
    introduction, 137
    jargon and clichés, avoiding, 140
    pitfalls, avoiding, 142–52
    quotations, 138–39
    revise and proofread, 152
    style, 139
    tense, 140–41
    thesis, stating, 137–38
    title, 137
    voice, 140
Reliability, of evidence, 14–15
Research
    paper journal, 102
    paper schedule, 101–2
    planning, 100–102
    tentative outline for, 101
    writing and, 12–13
Research Navigator, 73
Research papers
    bibliography, 99–100
    body, 112–14
    conclusion, 114
    final draft, 115
    finding sources, 102–6
    first draft, 115
    introductions, 109–12
    notetaking, 106–8
    organizing, 109–14
    outline for, 114
    proofreading, 115
    revisions, 115

subject selection, 97–99
tracking research, 100–102
writing, 97–115
Resource trail, creating, 106
*Retreat of the Elephants: An Environmental
    History of China* (Elvin), 19
reverend, 149
Reviews
    book, 92–96
    of facts, 25
    organizing, 93–94
    of textbooks, 31
    writing, 93–94
Revision, 152
    of research paper, 115
    of short papers, 82–83
RLG Union Catalog, 72–73
Roman numerals, in notetaking, 33
Roosevelt, Franklin D., 13
Run-on sentences, 149–50

S

Saikku, Mikko, 19
Salem witchcraft trials, 12
Santayana, George, 5
Schedule
    for research paper, 101–2
    for study, 25
Search engines, 69–71
Search Engine Watch, 70
Sensitivity, toward classmates, 52
Sensory memory, 24
Sentence
    fragments, 150
    run-on, 149–50
serve, service, 150
share, 150
Shorter, Edward, 18
Short essays, writing, 83–84
Short papers
    drafting thesis, 80
    final draft, 83
    first draft, 81–82
    organizing, 80–81
    revising, 82–83
    writing, 78–96
Short-term memory, 24
*should of, might of, could of, should of, would
    of,* 144
sight, site, cite, 150
Simmons, I.G., 19
Simplicity, in writing, 139
Slavery, study of, 19

Social Science Index, 72, 103
Social Scisearch, 72, 103
Sources
  background material, 102–3
  books, 103
  citing, 114–35
  finding, 102–6
  Internet material, 103–4
  periodical, 103
  primary, 104–6
  resource trail, 106
special, 150
Speech, 53
Spodek, Howard, 23
Stalin, Josef, 43
Strategies, for taking tests, 59
Study. *See* Effective study
Studying, for tests, 56–59
Subject selection, for research papers, 97–99
Subject-verb agreement, 151
such that, 151

T

task, as verb, 151
Tentative outline, 101
Tests, 57
  during, 59–63
  answering questions on, 59–63
  important points on, 56–57
  organization of information for, 57–58
  plotting strategies for, 59
  preparation for, 58
  principles of good English, 59
  studying for, 56–59
  success with, 56–63
  time management and, 58–59
Textbooks, 26–31
  important points, identify, 27–29
  learning techniques, 29–31
  review, 31
  survey material in, 26
  themes in, 23
that, who, which, 152
there, their, 151
Thernstrom, Stephen, 18
Thesis
  bibliographies for, 135
  citing, 128–29
  drafting, 80, 85
  stating, 137–38
Thesis statement, 23
  developing, 95

This Delta, This Land: An Environmental History of the Yazoo-Mississippi Floodplain (Saikku), 19
Thompson, E.P., 18
Thucydides, 17
Time management, 25
  for tests, 58–59
  schedule, importance of, 25
Title, including, 137
to, too, two, 151
Topic, narrowing, 98
Town in the Ruhr: A Social History of Bochum (Crew), 18
Trevor-Roper, Hugh, 14
The Triumph of Will, 48
True-false questions, 63
Turabian, Kate L., 119

U

Ulrich, Laura Thatcher, 13, 18
Ulrich's International Periodicals Directory, 105
unique, 152
URL (uniform resource locator), 67

V

Verbs, past tense of, 140–41
very, 152
Videotapes, study of, 46–48
Virtual office hours, 65
Voice, active *versus* passive, 140
von Ranke, Leopold, 17

W

Washington, George, 28
Web sites
  bibliographies for, 135
  citing, 130–31
  content of, 69
  evaluating, 67–69
  history, 75–77
  publishers', 75
Webster, Daniel, 54
who, which, that, 152
whose, who's, 152
Wills, Garry, 11
Women at Work (Dublin), 18
Women's history, 19
World War I, 7
World War II, 16
World Wide Web, 64, 65, 67–69
  evaluating web sites, 67–69
Worster, Donald, 19

would of, might of, could of, should of,
    should of, 144
Writing
    book reviews, 92–96
    comparisons, 84–92
    conciseness of, 141–42
    efficiently, 79–83
    of test questions, 59
    reference guide for, 136–53
    research and, 12–13
    research papers, 97–115

short essays, 83–84
short papers, 78–96
simplicity in, 139
with degree of formality, 140

Y

Yahoo, 70

Z

Zeitgeschichte, 6